D1287680

Donna and Shannon Freeman

with Craig Boreth

THREE RIVERS PRESS • NEW YORK

SEVEN
STEPS

TO

SOLD

The secrets to selling your home
for big bucks . . . **FAST!**

Three Rivers Press and the Tugboat design are registered trademarks of
Random House, Inc.

HGTV and the HGTV logo design are registered trademarks of Scripps Networks, LLC.
Used with permission. All rights reserved.

Library of Congress Cataloging-in-Publication Data
Freeman, Donna.
Seven steps to sold: the secrets to selling your home for big bucks . . . fast! /
Donna and Shannon Freeman; with Craig Boreth.
    p.   cm.
Includes index.
1. House selling.   2. Real estate business.   I. Freeman, Shannon.
II. Boreth, Craig.   III. Title.
HD 1379.F684   2007
643'.12—dc22   2006034886

ISBN 978-0-307-35187-6

Printed in the United States of America

DESIGN BY ELINA D. NUDELMAN
ILLUSTRATIONS BY FRANK PAINE

10 9 8 7 6 5 4 3 2 1

First Edition

To all of our clients, many of whom have spanned decades and generations. It is because of the knowledge that we gained from our experiences with each one of you that we were able to write this book. You are like extended family and we are grateful to have been involved in an important part of your lives.

Contents

Preface

Donna: We've been in this business a long time. A *really* long time.

Shannon: Yeah, when Mom got her real estate license, it was written on a stone tablet.

Donna: That's my daughter, ladies and gentlemen. Isn't she fantastic? But seriously, we have learned so much over the years. And we were still shocked when we started writing this book and actually realized just what goes into each and every real estate transaction.

Shannon: And it's even more shocking when we remind ourselves that there's at least one surprise in every new transaction we close (and usually many more).

Donna: Right. Each time I think I've earned the right to know everything, I have to learn something new. Hopefully when you're finished with this book, you'll know a whole lot more about selling your home, but you'll also understand that you can never know everything.

Shannon: Exactly. You really have to be open minded and a little bit adventurous, because anything can happen. Our most flexible clients are usually the most successful. Clients who dig in their heels sometimes just end up getting dragged through the mud.

Donna: Speaking of mud, we've got a story about a stack of bricks that might help you appreciate everything that goes into a successful sale. How's that for a change of subject?

Shannon: Very smooth, Mom. It's a little parable we like to call "It All Adds Up."

A Seller's Parable—
It All Adds Up

IMAGINE THAT you've already sold your house. You've done all the hard work, negotiated the best possible deal, and made a clean break emotionally with your old home. You can finally sit down and calculate how you did. Best-case scenario, you're happy with the sale price, and you feel like your agent was well worth his or her commission. After you factor in the other closing costs, repairs, and whatever value you'd like to place on any unexpected delays or emotional wear and tear, you can determine the net outcome of the whole adventure.

Now imagine that dollar amount as a stack of bricks reaching (hopefully) way up toward the sky. If you just sold a place in Manhattan or Beverly Hills, you may want to imagine them as solid gold bricks. For the rest of us, just regular old bricks will do. Those bricks represent all of the factors that determined the final value of your house. Some things—like the location and the physical structure of the house—account for many of the bricks. Other factors—like replacing the doormats, shampooing the rugs, and all of the countless other things you can do to ensure a good sale—might account for a single brick or just a few. The point is, whether those factors are really important (like the current market conditions) or just barely noticeable (like the condition of your toilet seats), they all add up to determine the success of your sale. It's not as if your house won't sell unless you do everything we recommend in this book. But the more you can do, the more likely it will be that you'll attract the most qualified buyers and get them to offer the most money in the least amount of time.

The flip side is that any mistakes can send lots of bricks tumbling from the stack, representing real money taken out of your pocket. Selling your home is a big deal, probably the largest single financial transaction you'll ever undertake. While that fact shouldn't intimidate you, you do need to realize that even a seemingly insignificant oversight can knock out lots of bricks. More important, as our society gets more and more litigious, a simple mistake can land you in court on the wrong side of a devastating lawsuit. But there's plenty of time for us to share horror stories. For now let's focus on the positive, since the goal of this book is to give you the knowledge and the tools you'll need to build the tallest stack of bricks possible.

99 Simple Ways to Ensure a Successful Sale

We want to make sure you get your money's worth from this book, so to start things off, here's a list of ninety-nine things you can do to improve your chances of a successful sale. If you follow just a handful of the suggestions on this list, we're confident that you'll improve the net value of your home enough to buy copies of this book for all of your friends. We'll talk about some of these suggestions in more detail later, but we hope you'll get a few good ideas from the list and get started right now on the road to SOLD.

Many of these suggestions may seem obvious, but since there's so much to keep track of, we figured it would be helpful to include them anyway. Some suggestions may seem ridiculous. But trust us, they work. We're sure you can come up with lots of other ideas, so just use this list as a guide to get started.

As soon as possible . . .

1. *Start packing! You should begin the moving-out process the minute you decide to sell.*

2. *Stack packed boxes neatly in the garage.*

3. *Flip through different home decor magazines and pay attention to room layouts and colors to get a sense of what's in style.*

4. *Go to local open houses to see what's on the market and how they've prepared their homes for sale.*

5. *Visit a model home to see the ultimate example of staging.*

6. *Start thinking about your schedule, particularly when you'll want to be completely moved out.*

7. *Remember what you loved about the house when you first saw it.*

8. *Take a moment to appreciate how valuable your house has been as a home, not just as an investment.*

9. *Start to move out mentally, and think of your home as a commodity (see our Second Rule of Real Estate in the introduction).*

10. *Start reading the Real Estate section of your local newspaper.*

11. *Thin out your wardrobe and donate to Goodwill.*

12. *Find a place for everything, and put everything in its place. Anything without a place either gets thrown out, goes into storage, or gets donated.*

continued

13. Have a garage sale. Make sure that unwanted or unusable items are priced to sell.

14. Check out www.zillow.com for current home values in your area.

15. Find the perfect real estate agent for you (see Step 2).

16. Do a complete staging walk through with your real estate agent or another objective person to determine what you need to do to get your house ready for the market (see Step 4 and Step 5).

17. If you're planning on buying new furniture after you move, consider buying it now and refurnishing your current place. The same goes for linens, area rugs, and curtains.

18. Dig up your old home inspection from when you bought your house and see if there's anything you haven't addressed.

19. Hire an inspector to do a preemptive inspection.

20. Figure out your monthly utility bills to give to buyers if asked. This shows you're organized.

21. Find a good accountant, if you don't already have one.

22. Consider making your home more energy efficient with high-efficiency appliances, new windows, or better insulation, or even just a programmable thermostat. (A 1998 study by the EPA found that a home's value rises an average of $20 for each $1 decrease in the annual utility bill.)

23. If you're buying another house, make sure you're preapproved for your mortgage.

24. Think about any problems you've had with the house, and get ready to disclose them or think about repairing them.

25. If you're taking out a home improvement loan or financing your next home,

check your credit report and make sure it's correct (see Resources for Sellers, page 223).

26. Find pictures showing the house in different seasons (particularly if it's on the market in the winter).

Shortly before your house is on the market . . .

27. Make sure all the doors have working doorstops.

28. Replace any old outlet or light switch covers. Get the white ones, not the almond ones, which look old even when they're new.

29. Make sure all the toilets flush correctly (if not, see Step 4).

30. Add 2000 Flushes automatic toilet bowl cleaners to every toilet.

31. Clean out and organize the cabinet under the kitchen sink (for some reason, almost all guys look under there).

32. Test the ground fault interrupter (GFI) circuits in your bathrooms and kitchen. When you press Test, there should no longer be any power at the outlet. If there is power, call an electrician. Press Reset to return power to the outlet.

33. Put a new doormat by every exterior door.

34. Check all accessible drains for leaks (see Step 4 for repair tips).

35. Replace old showerheads, or make sure newer ones don't leak.

36. Set the water heater to 120°F. Anyone washing their hands should get warm water, but you don't want to burn them (plus, it saves money).

37. Hose down your house (hopefully just the outside needs it).

38. Replace your house number, or at least be sure it's clearly visible from the street.

39. Vacuum every corner and behind all furniture.

continued

40. Dust the tops of all doors, windows, picture frames, and so on.

41. Vacuum the bugs out of every outdoor light fixture.

42. Line up all your books neatly (maybe even in order).

43. Use half a walnut to hide scratches on furniture or flooring (see Step 4 for other renewal tips).

44. Fertilize the grass, add new mulch outside, and trim indoor plants.

45. Replace all burned-out lightbulbs.

46. Replace the batteries in your smoke detectors (it's a good idea anyway).

47. Replace your cabinet and drawer pulls.

48. Make sure all clocks are working (replace batteries as necessary) and set to the correct time.

49. Remove any books, art, or photos that may be considered controversial or offensive.

50. Remove any extreme political materials.

51. Empty the garage. Throw away or donate what you can, sweep the floor, and then put everything back neatly.

52. Clean up any oil spills on the driveway or garage floor.

53. Make sure all potentially embarrassing items, everything from prescriptions to certain types of magazines (hint, hint), are removed from accessible drawers.

54. Remove half of your personal photos; then remove half of those that are left. Fill in any nail holes in the walls (see Step 4).

55. Spray silicone spray (not WD-40) on all squeaky or tight hinges, sliding door tracks, and so forth.

56. Organize the extension cords for your computer, stereo, and other appliances.

57. Get some lightly scented air fresheners (Glade Clean Linen scent is perfect).

58. Remove everything you've stuck onto the refrigerator. Empty the refrigerator and every drawer and cabinet, throw away anything you don't want, and put the remaining things back neatly.

59. Put one potted herb in the kitchen (we suggest rosemary, which is hearty and smells great).

60. Buy nice wooden hangers for your clothes.

61. Get some cedar for your closets (Bed Bath & Beyond has some you just hang with your clothes).

62. If you have a fireplace, vacuum it out and put in fresh logs.

63. Buy a cookbook stand, and place your nicest cookbook in it, open to a particularly beautiful recipe.

64. Take a level around the house and level off all the frames, mirrors, and so on.

65. Set your lawn mower so that it only cuts the top third of the grass, which will promote a healthy lawn.

66. See what parts of your house are hit by direct sunlight during the early afternoon (when open houses are most likely to occur). Make sure those places are spotless, since the sun will illuminate every bit of dust.

67. Replace the air filter in your furnace.

68. Clean the kitchen floor with a sponge (it's the only way you'll really see just how dirty it is).

69. Make sure your front door key works smoothly. If not, either spray the lock with silicone spray or replace the doorknob completely.

70. Tell people that your house is for sale.

continued

71. Get a Dustbuster for quick cleanups whenever necessary.

72. Get the carpets steam-cleaned.

73. Cut back any exterior plants that are blocking sunlight into the house.

74. If you have cats, get a covered litter box and find a discreet place for it and the food.

75. If you have dogs, make plans to contain them, or better yet get them out of the house during showings (same thing for unruly cats, too). Also, make sure there's no poop in the yard. While we're on the subject, you might also want to avoid letting your dog pee on the grass, since the high pH and nitrogen level of dog urine (particularly from female dogs) is bad for the grass.

76. Make sure every door is easily accessible from both sides.

77. Wash the windows (see Step 5 for instructions).

78. Clean out everything from under the beds.

79. Make a CD of classy, pleasant music to play during showings. Classical guitar is usually a safe bet (and you can't go wrong with Segovia).

80. Have your chimney swept.

81. Make sure all of your windows open (and don't slam shut when you let go).

Just before the open house . . .

82. Make sure the lights are on for every showing.

83. Put new toilet paper rolls in all the bathrooms.

84. Put new soaps at all the sinks and showers.

85. Put fresh flowers and/or plants outside the front door.

86. Set the dining-room table.

87. Get rid of all dried flowers (see "Words from the Wise: The Feng Shui Lady" in Step 5).

88. Put fresh flowers in vases around the house.

89. Empty every trash can in the house.

90. Shake out/fluff up all bathroom/kitchen rugs.

91. Put a bowl of fresh fruit in the kitchen.

92. Grind half a lemon in your garbage disposal.

93. Wash all the sheets and towels and make the beds.

94. Spray your sheets with linen spray. Restoration Hardware (www.restorationhardware.com) has a scent called Fresh that's perfect.

95. Keep the kitchen sink and dishwasher empty. If there are dishes in the dishwasher, make sure you run the dishwasher before anyone arrives.

96. Open all the windows (weather permitting).

97. Open the window shades to let in as much natural light as possible (assuming the view is tolerable).

98. Close the shower curtains.

99. Clean like you've never cleaned before!

Introduction

RATHER THAN make you read this entire book to figure out what it's all about, we figured you'd want to get the essence of it right here in the introduction. So, without further ado, here is the Freemans' First Rule of Real Estate:

Living in your home and selling it are very different things

We know, it sounds obvious. But many of life's guidelines—like "Do unto others," "Turn the other cheek," and "Never try to teach a pig to sing"—only appear simple. The reality behind each statement (except maybe for the one about the pig) is actually quite complex.

The fact is that selling your home successfully requires a

pretty significant transformation on your part. You'll need to change both the way you live and the way you think. As you live in your home day after day, you become connected to it both physically and emotionally. Our homes become much more than mere shelters. They directly reflect almost everything about us, showcasing our family histories, our tastes in art, music and design, our hobbies, and just about every other facet of our personalities. In a very real sense *we are where we live.* But as we'll see, selling your home requires that you disconnect yourself from the very place with which you've spent years getting connected. It's not something that comes naturally to most of us, and it's not easy. That's where we come in.

We know how difficult it is to make that transition from homeowner to home seller, but we also know how essential that transition is to a successful and profitable sale. We don't expect people to make the leap right away, but hopefully as you make your way through this book, eventually you'll get there. Of course, we do anticipate a little push-back along the way (you wouldn't be a good seller if you didn't speak your mind). For example, when we suggest that you empty all of your trash cans every day that your house may be shown, you're likely to respond with something like: "Are you nuts?" People react this way because they have yet to make the switch from homeowner to home seller. Once you're firmly entrenched in home-seller mode, you'll see it as just another thing you've got to do to make the sale.

To help you along in the transition from homeowner to home seller, here's our Second Rule of Real Estate:

The moment you decide to sell your home, it's no longer your home. It's a commodity.

This rule might sound a little severe, but in the end it's a crucial step to success. A commodity in this sense is just some generic product that has value to you only because it can be sold, the way commodities traders sell pork bellies. You need to distance yourself emotionally from your home in order to sell it successfully. We've found that thinking about it this way really helps our clients make a clean break.

In contrast, when you're living in your home, you get value from it in all of the ways you use it. The longer you live in a house, the more personally invested you become in it and the more emotionally valuable it is to you. You put up more pictures; you know all of its little quirks. You know just how to jiggle the handle on the toilet to stop it from running and just the right way to get the windows to stay open. Simply put, your house becomes your home. When you go to sell your home, it needs to become just a house again. While your house is on the market, you need to do your best to forget about all the wonderful times you had there, how great it feels when someone walks in the door and compliments all of your personal touches, and how warm and cozy it makes you feel. The time has come to view this structure as a commodity. We know, it sounds so cold and cruel to abandon your home like that (for help on making a clean break, see Step 1). Just remember, someday soon it won't be yours anymore, and the more quickly and completely you make the break and the more thoroughly you master the Seven Steps to SOLD, the better off you'll be.

That Lived-in Look

Donna: I think when my time finally comes, I want my gravestone to say something about how living in your home is different from selling it. It's like one of the golden rules that I live by and expect all my clients to live by as well. For one thing, it takes some of the pressure off when your house isn't on the market and you don't feel like cleaning your house.

Shannon: She always uses it as an excuse when I come over for dinner. I'll say something like, "You think maybe you could've straightened up a bit for me?" and she'll immediately come back with, "Hey! My house isn't on the market. Cut me some slack."

Donna: She's right, actually. My house is usually a bit on the cluttered side. My kitchen table does double duty as a filing cabinet, the dish rack is terminally half full, and my superdog, Ruby, has free rein of the place. Whenever clients come over, particularly after I've given them a huge laundry list of chores for *their* homes, they inevitably make some comment about the mess. My answer to them is the same as to Shannon: "My house isn't on the market." I couldn't care less how people *live* in their homes, but when our clients put their homes on the market, it's a different ball game.

USING THIS BOOK

The ultimate goal of this book is to help you understand and live by the Freemans' Rules of Real Estate when you sell your house. Hopefully they'll help you stay sane, organized, and better prepared to have a successful sale. We've found in our more than forty years of combined experience that sellers who embrace these rules, and follow as many of our suggestions as possible, are much more likely to sell for more money in less time.

As we go through the Seven Steps to Sold, we'll discuss a countless number of strategies you *should* employ to help increase your chance of a successful sale. We don't expect anyone to do everything we recommend (although you probably could if you had the time and ambition), but we strongly encourage you to do as much as possible. We've really thrown everything but the kitchen sink into this book, hoping that anyone who reads it will get a lot of good suggestions for his or her own unique situation. The important thing to realize is that everything in this book, from the biggest decisions down to the tiniest details, is included to increase your chances of a successful sale.

As you decide which of our recommendations you can follow, just keep in mind that the more you do, the better off you're likely to be. When we think about how our clients' hard work can pay off, we always think back to when Shannon was a kid and was seriously into gymnastics. Her coach was tough and pushed the gymnasts hard. He always used to say, "The harder you work, the luckier you'll be." It's the same with selling your house. Many times when sellers have great success, they can't imagine how lucky they were that this particular buyer happened to drop by and make a great offer. In fact, that "lucky" outcome was the result of lots of hard work preparing the house for the market. We hope this book becomes every seller's good luck charm.

WHO THE BOOK IS FOR

We've written this book for just about *any* home sellers who want to set their goals high and have the most successful sale possible. We don't assume that you have much experience selling houses, although since you've probably been through the home-buying process, some of the information may be familiar.

One assumption we do make is that you will earn more from the sale of your home than you owe on your mortgage.

Selling a home for less than what's owed is known as a "short sell." This can certainly happen if home prices drop dramatically, and it may require that you pay the difference to your mortgage lender at the closing. This type of transaction can be quite complicated, and we simply do not have the space in this book to address it adequately. If you're facing a short sell, definitely discuss your options in detail with an experienced agent or real estate attorney.

Also, we just couldn't include a comprehensive tutorial for people who decide to go the "for sale by owner" (or FSBO, pronounced FIZZ-bo) route. While we truly believe that you'll be better off working with an experienced, professional real estate agent, we still respect people with the drive and determination to sell their homes themselves. FSBOs should find a lot of useful information in this book. In particular, we mention several critical steps in the process when FSBOs need to be really careful in order to avoid costly mistakes.

SPECIAL FEATURES

We've been in this business so long, and have internalized so much about it that it was quite a shock when we started brainstorming for this book (we prefer the more appropriate term brain-dumping) and actually thought about everything that's involved in selling a house. In particular, putting ourselves in a seller's shoes reminded us of just how maddening the whole process can be. We soon realized that the more that sellers know about the process, even those things you don't technically *need* to know, the better off you'll be. And, quite frankly, the better off your agent will be as well, since an educated seller is the best type of client.

Of course, organizing all of this information was a bit of a challenge. So we've created a few different features to include throughout the book to illustrate points, explain terms, or share interesting anecdotes.

Buzzword The real estate world is full of jargon. We use it so often when dealing with other agents that sometimes we don't even notice the perplexed looks on our clients' faces. Later on, when they ask us what in the world we were talking about, we realize that our shorthand went right over their heads. To help you translate agent-speak into normal human language, we'll define many of the most common terms that you might want to know.

No-Brainer We hope this book will be helpful to just about anyone who is selling their home. You may find that certain suggestions are completely obvious, whereas someone else may not. We'll present many of the most commonsense suggestions as "No-Brainers," both to help those sellers with less experience and to make sure that veteran sellers don't forget the fundamentals.

Top-Dollar Tip Certain suggestions in the book are designed to directly increase the sale price of your home. We'll see that there are many ways to define a successful sale, but price is almost always toward the top of the list. Use these tips to increase your chances of getting the best price.

Fool's Fable The average homeowner sells only two or three houses in his lifetime, so learning from your own mistakes is a bad idea. It's much better to learn from the mistakes of others. We include these true tales for both their educational and, many times, comedic value.

Buyer's Eyes   The home buyer is your customer, and understanding his or her needs and concerns is crucial to closing a successful sale. Step 3 will help you get inside the buyers' mind, but throughout the book we'll try to see things through their eyes.

Insider Secret   From your real estate agent to your mortgage broker to your movers, you'll encounter many experienced professionals along the way. We'll share their tricks of the trade to help make your sale a success.

Words from the Wise   Besides us real estate agents, there are many other people involved in the sales process. We've sat down with a bunch of them to get their perspectives and advice on the process.

We wish you the best of luck on the road to SOLD. We hope you exceed all of your goals, learn something about yourself, and maybe even have a little fun along the way.

1

Seller, Know Thyself

EVERY SALE we've ever closed has been unique—it's the individual personalities and goals of the clients that make each one so different. You might think that selling your house is all about the house, but in reality it's much more about you. And the more you understand your own situation, your personal approach to the process, and exactly what you want to get out of it, the more successful you'll be.

In this first step to SOLD, we'll encourage you to take a good, long look at yourself and see what kind of seller you are. What are your goals? How emotionally attached are you to your home? How will you set the schedule for your sale? And, just before we move to Step 2 and start looking for an agent, you'll figure out what kind of client you are so you'll be able to locate the best person to represent you. But first, let's start with a seemingly obvious question . . .

WHY ARE YOU SELLING?

The first question to ask yourself is, Why am I selling my house? The answer may be obvious, but it's worth thinking about because it will affect how you approach the process every step of the way. Here's a quick overview of the major categories of sellers. You may find that you fit into more than one category, in which case you should pay attention to the issues pertaining to each. Or, if you find your own situation isn't listed here, take a look at similar situations to find issues that may affect you.

Upsizing

This is the classic scenario of the growing young family moving to a bigger house to accommodate the kids. You need more bedrooms, more storage space, and a bigger garage. You may be looking for a bigger house for other reasons, such as a move from the city to the suburbs, but the situations are similar on the selling end.

Upsizing tends to be very stressful. First of all, there's the money. In most cases, upsizers are moving within the same market, so more space means a higher price. There's a dangerous tendency for upsizers to overprice their current homes because they're buying a more expensive one. *Be very careful not to let your future needs dictate your strategy for selling your current home.* Interestingly, we find that people who are upsizing to *cheaper* markets, and therefore feel less pressure on their current sale, seem to have the most successful sales.

Second, upsizing is stressful because it's usually not absolutely necessary. Sure, there are social pressures to buy the bigger house. It feels like something you *should* do. But you could survive perfectly fine within your current space if you absolutely had to. Psychologically, having a choice is more stressful than not having a choice, and upsizers can drive themselves crazy trying to decide if they're doing the right thing. On the other hand, upsizers tend to be less emotionally attached to their current homes. This move represents a big step forward in their lives, a new chapter that they're excited to embark on. Moving out emotionally tends to come pretty easily to these folks.

Downsizing

As the name suggests, downsizing is the opposite of upsizing, but in more ways than just square footage. The folks involved are usually older and the process itself tends to be less stressful, but the implications of the move can be very emotional. For example, suppose your kids are all grown and you just can't keep up the big house, or perhaps you need to live on one level because you just can't climb the stairs anymore. The decision to move is pretty simple—you have no choice. But admitting you're getting old and that this move may represent the final chapter of your life can be extremely difficult.

And then there's all the stuff. Downsizers have often lived in their homes for many, many years, and they've accumulated a treasure of personal items. What will you do with all this stuff? If you throw it away, are you throwing away your memories? And as we've said, the longer you stay in a house, the more attached you become to it, sometimes even to the structure itself. We once knew an older couple who put a clause in their sales agreement that if anyone ever tore the house down they wanted the wood! Even for downsizers who aren't that old, they're often moving away from homes where they watched their children grow up, and it's just as difficult to break away emotionally.

Finally, downsizers often have financial issues to address. If your house was paid off long ago, the sale may represent a huge capital gain. While this is a good thing, there are important tax implications to consider. As you may know, there is an exemption from federal tax on the first $250,000 ($500,000 for couples who file joint returns) on capital gains from the sale of your primary residence (for more information, see "Let's Talk Taxes" in Step 6). Above that, the tax can hit pretty hard. You should definitely talk to an accountant to make sure you minimize your tax burden.

There are also downsizers who are moving back into a city. These folks—while usually "empty nesters" possibly facing similar financial issues—often can't wait to get back to the vibrant life of the city and don't face the same emotional challenges.

Death or Divorce

Sellers in these situations face both high stress and powerful emotions. It goes without saying that you should hire a lawyer and an accountant (and probably a good therapist as well) to help you get through either scenario.

Selling the home of a deceased family member is never simple. You would be amazed at how quickly people come out of the woodwork and get involved. Selling a home under normal circumstances is difficult enough. Doing it by committee with all the added emotions is almost impossible. It is essential that you work toward the smoothest possible transaction because as soon as conflicts start to arise they tend to snowball out of control.

Selling a home as part of a divorce tends to be as simple or as complicated as the settlement itself. The risk, of course, is that one party will sabotage the sale for the other. We've seen spouses refuse to vacate the property or intentionally damage the house. If you're in a divorce situation, just make sure to keep in mind that the house, as your largest asset, is also likely to be one of the largest sources of conflict.

Change of Job

Surveys often find the top four most stressful life events to be death, marriage, moving, and changing jobs. So sellers in this group are facing two of the top four at the same time.

Your first priority here should be getting buy-in from the entire family. You may be moving to a new city, putting your kids in a new school, and doing it all in a relatively short period of time. If everyone isn't on board from the beginning, you'll be facing a constant uphill struggle.

Besides family consensus, timing is the other crucial factor for these folks. Many times one parent will go ahead to the new city while the other stays home with the family. You need to find a new house in a new city, while selling your current house on a tight schedule. This is definitely one of the most difficult situations for sellers to face.

External Factors

Occasionally we have clients who sell because the neighborhood has changed around them and they can no longer stay there. Or they move to get into a better school district. These and other issues not specifically related to the house itself can cause problems for sellers, particularly if the problems require disclosure.

For example, if there are nighttime noise issues that you just can't stand, you'll need to disclose them to the buyer. Otherwise, you could very easily be sued when the buyer discovers the nuisance. You might think that disclosing such problems would lower the value of your house, and you would be right. But this is not something you can hide from buyers, so you'll just have to decide if moving away from the problem is worth it for you.

Just to See . . .

It's been years since we've agreed to represent clients who wanted to put their house on the market "just to see" what would happen. Then, if they received a high enough offer, they'd sell. It might be obvious to you that this is a bad idea, but the reasons why it's a bad idea can provide some interesting insight into the process.

First of all, sellers who just want to see what will happen are obviously not serious about selling, so they won't do everything they should to prepare their house for the market. As a consequence, their agent is likely to be less experienced, since seasoned agents wouldn't accept these clients in the first place. The end result is that the sellers are unlikely to get a high enough bid to sell. They might think to themselves, "No problem, I'll just take it off the market and relist it later." Big problem.

We can't emphasize strongly enough that putting your house on the market is not a risk-free proposition. You can't just list it, take it off the market, and then relist it as if nothing happened. Real estate agents have long memories, and they'll remember that at one time you were not a serious seller. This memory could deter them from enthusiastically showing your home to their potential buyer.

Second, these folks often consider selling their house because the market is hot and they can cash out and make a big profit. That's fine if you're a real estate investor, but most of us think of our house as a home first and an investment second (see "The Seller Profiles" opposite). One risk of suddenly thinking like an investor is that you may be underestimating the emotional value of your home. If you do end up getting a high enough offer, that probably means the entire market is overheated, so you might tuck your proceeds away and wait for the market to settle down before buying again. That means renting for a while. Have you thought about how it will feel to be a tenant again? Specifically, have you forgotten how great it felt when you finally owned your own place? That's a valuable feeling and should not be overlooked. There are other risks to thinking like an investor, namely that you may be taking on more personal and financial risk than you can afford to, or you simply may not appreciate just how much of an inconvenience selling your house and moving out can be.

The Seller Profiles

You can think of your house as a home or as an investment, or some combination of the two. The groupings below illustrate how people feel differently about their homes.

The first group—the Homebodies—includes people who think of their houses almost exclusively as homes. They just love their homes and make them exactly as they want them to be. They don't care about resale value and hardly ever even entertain the notion of selling at all.

The second group—the Money Men (and Women)—includes people who consider their homes purely as investments. They carefully consider any renovations, keeping a close eye on the local market. They don't get personally attached to their homes. These are people who essentially live in model homes, waiting for the right moment to sell for maximum profit.

The third group—the Domestic Investors—includes people who love their homes just as much as Homebodies do, but also think very carefully about them as investments, like Money Men. These folks probably have a very personal sense of decor in the house but do upgrades and renovations with an eye to resale.

We also assume that there are people, although we've never actually met any, who are neither personally nor financially invested in their homes. For these people— let's call them the Castaways—a house is just a shelter.

Most of us are probably Homebodies, especially when our houses are not on the market. But the most successful sellers are usually Money Men or Domestic Investors. It's worthwhile to take a moment and consider which group you're in and how you might need to adapt your thinking to be a better seller. Also, if you're married or you're selling with a partner, do you both think about the house in the same way? If not, you're likely to approach the process of selling it rather differently. So talk it over and make sure you're on the same page as you move forward.

WHAT ARE YOUR GOALS?

- -

If you don't know where you're going,
you'll end up somewhere else.
—Alfred Adler

- -

Quick, what's your number-one goal in selling your house? We'll bet your answer had something to do with money, either making the most amount of money, selling for a certain price, or netting enough to live large in the Caymans now that the kids have all graduated and moved out. When we ask new clients this question, we get pretty much the same answer. Our follow-up question is always, Are you sure about that?

Setting realistic, appropriate goals is an important exercise for two reasons. First of all, the only real way to gauge a successful sale is to measure the outcome against the goals you set for yourself. Second, setting your goals helps you remain focused on the truly important outcomes of the sale, and avoid being distracted along the way. Your goals help you select the best agent, set your schedule, and negotiate the deal that works best for you. First, we'll do a little exercise to help you get a sense of what your goals are. Then we'll explore each of those goals in detail and look at their potential consequences. After that we'll do the same exercise again to see if our advice has changed your goals at all.

RANK YOUR GOALS

Here's a list of the most common goals we see in sellers. Rank them in order from most important to the least important (with 1 being the most important). If you value multiple goals equally, give them the same ranking. Add in any other goals you might have and rank them as well. If you're selling your house as part of a couple, both of you should rank your own goals and then compare them.

___ Make the most money

___ Sell quickly

___ Time the sale with a purchase (concurrent closing)

___ Have a smooth transaction

___ Find the right buyers

___ Put the best product on the market

___ Other goal: _____

___ Other goal: _____

___ Other goal: _____

Goal 1: Make the Most Money

Since this goal is obviously on everybody's mind, we'll address it first. Of course, if you're thinking about your home as a commodity, you want to sell it for the maximum amount possible. The question you need to ask yourself is, What risks am I taking on by *only* focusing on getting top dollar? In our experience, the single most common mistake sellers make is underestimating the risks involved in the process. That's why we recommend getting a good agent, and that's why it's important to realize that if you want the biggest reward, you're probably going to be taking the biggest risks.

Our favorite real estate lawyer, Steven Spierer (see "Words from the Wise: The Lawyer" in Step 6), has a great analogy for people who don't understand risk. "It's just like people who drive without their seat belts," he likes to say. "They'll exclaim with great pride that they've never worn a seat belt, and it hasn't hurt them yet. But as you're hurtling headfirst through the windshield, it's a bad time to think about putting on your seat belt." Take appropriate precautions ahead of time; once the damage is done there's no going back.

Here's how placing the profit goal above all others can easily get you in trouble. When we discuss setting the listing price for your house (see Step 2), we'll see that setting the price too high can cause real problems. This is exactly the mistake made by people who focus exclusively on getting the highest price. We've had clients get bids that were 5 percent or even 10 percent above the next highest bid. We can recognize the look in their eyes the moment they see the dollar amount on the page, and we know we've got our work cut out for us. You need to take a long, hard look at just how serious that offer is and how solid the financial data are that back it up. The risk here is that the offer could fall through, and then you've got to relist the house with the stigma of the defunct deal. As we'll see in "Setting the Listing Price" in Step 2, nothing has changed with the house itself, but in all but the hottest sellers' markets, prospective buyers will always wonder why that first deal fell through, and they'll be much more skeptical and aggressive negotiators.

There's also a timing issue to consider. For example, suppose you put your house on the market in June and you accept an offer in July. If the deal falls through in August, you have to relist in September. As we'll see in Step 3, there's definitely a high season for home buyers, and September is not a part of it. We knew of a house that received an offer well above asking price, but the deal fell through just before Christmas. The sellers were stuck relisting in the dead of winter and eventually sold for well below their original asking price.

Just to be clear, we're not saying that you shouldn't do everything possible to get the most money for your house. In many cases the highest offer is the best one, and should be accepted. But receiving an offer and closing the sale are two different things, and selecting an unsound offer just because it is the highest is a risky venture indeed.

There are several questions you'll need to ask yourself if you're still all about the money.

1. *Am I willing to take the risk?* Buyers can bail out for any number of reasons at just about any point along the way. The sellers, though, have a much tougher time backing out (see Step 6). If you overlook potential problems with the highest offer, you're asking for trouble down the road that can cost you big bucks. It might work out fine, but make sure you're comfortable with the risks before you accept.

2. *Why exactly do I want to accept this offer?* Almost everyone wants more money, so obviously you want to get the most money for your house. Just make sure you don't let pride cloud your judgment. We're all proud of our accomplishments, but in this case you've got to be careful not to let your pride lead you into a bad deal. It's sort of like people who travel just so that they can tell people where they've been, rather than enjoy the experience of traveling. If you just can't wait to tell everyone how much you got for your house, you're probably not thinking clearly enough. When selling your house, try not to be competitive with your neighbors or your family. Stay focused on your own situation, and do what's best for you.

3. *Why is this person offering so much?* You've probably heard the old expression "If something seems too good to be true, it usually is." Well, it's worth keeping that in mind as you sell your house. Let's face it,

nobody will give you more money out of the goodness of their hearts. With the exception of the hottest markets, exemplified by multiple offers and bidding wars, you're unlikely to receive a substantially higher offer than you'd expect unless that buyer is trying to compensate for other things (such as bad credit, no down payment, or a late closing date).

Some sellers also believe that they'll encounter what we like to call the *Beverly Hillbillies* scenario. Nobody is going to roll into town and offer you way above market value for your house unless he just struck oil back in the hills. In other words, unless he's paying cash or putting up a huge down payment, you shouldn't take him seriously. Why not? One word: appraisal. The buyer's lender will appraise your house using much the same technique as agents use to set the listing price. Therefore, the buyer is going to have a tough time getting a mortgage for more than the property is actually worth.

4. What's my bottom line? We'll show you how to calculate your bottom line in Step 6. For now it's just good to realize that your actual bottom line—the lowest price you could confidently accept as the best option—is probably lower than you think. Knowing your bottom line can help free you from focusing too much on your listing price and open your eyes to all of the other factors that can add or subtract value from the final outcome.

Goal 2: Sell Quickly

Remember how we ask everyone if they are sure their number-one goal is to make the most money from the sale of their house? Well, as soon as we start talking about their time constraints, they realize that they're not so sure after all. They may think that they want the most money, but they've got to be at the new job on a certain date or the kids start school right after Labor Day. Unfortunately, you can't have it both ways. Something's got to give.

If you're on a tight schedule, you've got to price your house accordingly. Like it or not, you are a "motivated seller," the kind that makes bargain-hunting buyers giddy with anticipation. Be sure to discuss with your agent exactly when you need to be out of your house so you can work together as efficiently as possible (see "What's Your Schedule?" on page 44).

A tight schedule will also affect how you approach renovations and repairs (see Step 4). You'll probably need to limit yourself to fixing just the most visible problems and then disclose everything else. If the buyer requests additional repairs, you could plan to offer a credit back for those items. Also, a preemptive home inspection would definitely help with a quick sell—that way you'll know exactly what the repair issues are and you can plan accordingly.

Goal 3: Concurrent Closing

Coordinating the sale of your current house with the purchase of a new one can be tricky and can get really messy if you're not careful from the beginning. We visualize sellers in this situation as if they're suspended from a trapeze, desperately holding on to one bar with their hands and the other with their feet. They can't sell their current home until they find the new one, but they don't want to buy a new home until they sell their current one. Sellers usually get into trouble either when they find their new home and have to drop the price on their current one, or their current home sells and they're suddenly scrambling to find a new house to buy. This is a situation where flexibility and a good agent are absolutely essential.

A good agent will figure out the best way to accommodate your situation and make sure your house doesn't sit on the

Diamonds to Doughnuts

Just when we thought we'd seen it all, we get a bid that's almost 10 percent higher than the next highest bid. Our client is understandably interested. There's just one catch: the buyer wants to use diamonds as a down payment. We imagined a scene out of *Marathon Man*, with the buyer's agent arriving at our offices with a black attaché case handcuffed to his wrist. I think we can make a blanket generalization that anytime someone wants to give you something from a briefcase to which they are manacled, do not accept it. Luckily, our client was no fool, and neither were we, and we accepted a lower bid. The rest of the deal went smoothly, and our client never expressed any regrets.

FOOL'S FABLE

market for too long (what's known as getting "shelf stale") and you don't have to push back the closing date (which just means there's more time for something to go wrong with the deal).

This goal also tends to be important for people selling income properties, since there are financial implications that require them to buy a new place within a certain amount of time if they want to avoid paying capital gains taxes on the sale (see "Let's Talk Taxes" in Step 6). In this case, making sure the closings occur within the necessary time frame can save the seller thousands of dollars in taxes.

Do You Two Even Know Each Other?

Somehow, husbands and wives can bicker over a few dollars here and a few dollars there, but when there are potentially hundreds of thousands of dollars on the line, they won't take the time to sit down and discuss their goals. One of the most common goals they're not discussing is timing. We all know the old stereotype that husbands are always ready to leave the house before their wives. We've often seen the same disconnect between couples when they're selling a home. It is essential that you get on the same page with your partner and figure out which goals are most important to each of you.

NO-BRAINER

Goal 4: Have a Smooth Transaction

It's hard to put a dollar amount on peace of mind, but in our experience sellers who put this high on their list of goals end up satisfied with the outcome. We're not talking about sticking your head in the sand and living in blissful ignorance. Working for a smooth transaction means doing your homework, finding your perfect agent, and remaining flexible throughout the process. You'd think that going this route would mean rolling over and selling for less money, but we find more often than not that these are the sellers who ultimately do the best financially as well.

A related goal for these folks is to end up with a happy buyer. That doesn't mean you give them everything they ask for, but that the end result is a fair deal for everyone involved. We'll explore this idea in more detail when we talk about negotiation (see Step 6).

Goal 5: Find the Right Buyers

We've definitely had clients who were concerned about the type of person who would buy their house. This occurs for any number of reasons, but it's really an example of letting your emotions sway your decision. We're not saying that you should sell out your principles for a few bucks, but understand that if you put conditions on the type of person you'll sell to, you're limiting your field of potential buyers, which most likely will lead to a lower sale price and longer market time. We've heard of people who wouldn't sell because the buyers didn't like dogs, or smoked, or just hated the wallpaper. (How dare they!)

Sometimes, though, the sellers worry about how the new buyer will impact their neighbors. This is a legitimate concern, particularly if you're very close with your neighbors, and imagine that you will remain so. You need to ask yourself how much that good karma is worth to you, and ultimately make the decision based on your own goals and values.

Goal 6: Put the Best Product on the Market

We're always a bit surprised when we encounter sellers who have this as one of their top goals. These are people who just have a profound pride in their home, and it's important to them that the product they put on the market is of the highest possible quality. They're not overly concerned about the sale price or timing; they just love the idea of creating something that will be appreciated by the outside world.

If this goal seems ridiculous to you, it's worth taking a moment to give it some thought because you can use it

The Market Has a Mind of Its Own

One of the most dangerous mistakes sellers make is to determine how much they need to sell their house for in order to afford their next place. Unfortunately, your house is worth exactly what the market will bear, not a penny more or less. The market doesn't care that you're moving to a more expensive city and need more money for a down payment. What happens in these cases is the seller gets a number in his head and everything then revolves around that. The first big mistake the seller makes is to set the listing price based on this figure. As we'll see in the next chapter, there are very specific criteria used to set the listing price, and there are serious consequences for setting it incorrectly.

Generally, though, the biggest problem with predetermining the price you need is that it ties you to the process emotionally. And that's a bad place to be.

FOOL'S FABLE

to your advantage. Sellers who have this as a goal tend to do a great job preparing their homes for the market and they do end up getting top dollar. After all, they're really just being customer-focused, which is always a good thing when you're selling something. Of course, they may have invested quite a bit up front in preparing their homes for sale, but they get so much pleasure out of the process that it tends to be a rewarding experience for them from beginning to end.

RANK YOUR GOALS AGAIN

Now that you've given some thought to the implications of your goals, rank them again and see if you've made any changes.

___ Make the most money

___ Sell quickly

___ Time the sale with a purchase (concurrent closing)

___ Have a smooth transaction

___ Find the right buyers

___ Put the best product on the market

___ Other goal:_____

___ Other goal:_____

___ Other goal:_____

Most likely, if you ranked money first originally, you'll probably still do so. But perhaps now some of the more practical goals are coming in a close second or are tied for first. That doesn't mean you're condemned to selling your home for less than you'd like. It just means that you're taking a more careful, comprehensive approach to the process, and in fact you may even end up making more.

Keep these goals in mind as you interview potential agents, and get a sense of how their approach to the process will resonate or conflict with your own. After you select an agent, be sure to discuss your goals with him or her. That way, your agent can adjust his or her approach to make sure you meet or exceed your goals.

Visualization Exercise

Warning: The following may seem a bit weird (frankly, we find it a bit weird, and we live in Southern California). But as long as you do all the other hard work involved in selling your house, we figure a little mystical mind play is like chicken soup: it can't hurt.

Athletes in virtually every sport—from golf to diving to darts—use visualization to go through the motions in their minds and improve their performance. The idea is that if you allow your brain to "see" how to hit the ball or complete the dive or throw the dart, when it comes time to actually do those things you'll be better prepared. The same is true when selling your house.

Now that you know your goals, you can imagine what it will be like to go through the process of selling your house and accomplishing all of those goals. And we actually want you to visualize it playing out in your mind. Here's how to do it:

- *Sit or lie down in a comfortable position and close your eyes.*

- *Take a few deep breaths and allow yourself to relax.*

- *In your mind's eye, visualize the letter A or another innocuous symbol.*

- *Allow the letter to fade away, and replace it with the scene of selling your house. Imagine a perfectly clean and staged house. It's a beautiful day and the buyers are visiting the house and talking about how much they love it. You've taken care of everything, so there's no stress or pressure; it's all working out just as you'd hoped.*

- *When you're through with this scene, allow it to fade away and replace it with the letter A again. Keep breathing and remain relaxed.*

- *When you're ready, allow the letter to fade away and open your eyes.*

As you practice this visualization, it should feel more and more possible to make it a reality.

EMOTIONAL INVENTORY: ARE YOU HOOKED ON YOUR HOME?

As we've already noted, one of the most important parts of a successful sale is distancing yourself emotionally from your home. To help you understand just how attached you are to your home (and therefore to know how hard it will be for you to disconnect), we've devised a system for taking an emotional inventory of your home. Start with 100 points, and add or subtract points based on your answers.

1. *How many items in your house give you goosebumps?*
    a. More than five (+5)
    b. One to four (+2)
    c. Zero (-1)
    d. What on earth are you talking about? (-3)

2. *How much is your home an expression of who you are?*
    a. The doorbell plays our wedding song. (+5)
    b. The color scheme is based on a vision you once had at a Grateful Dead show in 1974. (+4)
    c. Your wedding picture is on display, but somewhere other than on the mantel, atop the television, or in every bathroom. (0)
    d. When your in-laws drop by, they think they've walked into the wrong house because they can't find any evidence that it's your house. They turn around and head back home (while you're hiding in the basement). (-3)

3. *How many personal items do you have stuck to your fridge?*
    a. There's a fridge behind all that stuff? (+5)
    b. Do drawings on the fridge itself count? (+3)
    c. My fridge is stainless steel and perfectly clean, so please don't touch it. (-1)

4. *Does your house have a name?* (+5)

5. *Did you* name the house? (+3)

6. *Do you have any framed photographs in your house that still have the pictures of the people that came with the frames?* (-5)

7. *How prominently featured are your collections?*
   a. They're all tucked away in the Hand-Painted Figurine annex upstairs. (+8)
   b. I've decorated the living room around my snow globes. (+5)
   c. My collection is stored safely in the garage. (-1)
   d. Any time I see an adult with a big collection on display, it reminds me of that house in *The Silence of the Lambs.* (-3)

8. *When someone visits your house for the first time, do you . . .*
   a. Take them on a two-hour tour, showing off all the framed photos of every trip you've taken since college? (+7)
   b. Tell them, "Yes, that is my wedding bouquet ensconced in Plexiglas above the fireplace?" (+5)
   c. Mix them a drink in the kitchen, while you recite the maximum BTUs of each burner on the stove and the cube-per-hour output of the automatic ice maker? (+3)
   d. Ask them if they'd like to make an offer on the place? (-3)

9. *When you move out of your house, what will you take?*
   a. The nails in the flooring, which your great-grandfather brought over from the old country hidden in a boiled ham (+6)
   b. Any plants currently in the ground (+5)
   c. Everything that's not nailed down (+3)

   d. If someone makes the right offer, I'll leave whatever they
      want. (-1)

   e. I won't even take the time to look back. Maui, here I
      come! (-3)

10. *What words do you use to describe your house?*
   a. Ethereal, vibrant, beguiling, rapturous (+4)
   b. Functional, perfect for us, utilitarian (+1)
   c. Disposable (-4)

11. *Would you refuse to sell your house to anyone . . .*
   a. Who would dismantle your exact replica of Princess Di's
      dressing chamber? (+5)
   b. Who would dare paint over the height chart on the
      kitchen wall? (+3)
   c. Who would immediately tear it down? (+1)
   d. Hey, if their money's green, I'm outta here. (-3)

12. *What happens when you imagine moving out?*
   a. It's like Charles Foster Kane calling out for his beloved
      Rosebud in *Citizen Kane.* (+5)
   b. I curl into a fetal position when I even think about
      everything that needs to be packed. (+2)
   c. Shhhh . . . I'm already gone. (-2)

13. *How difficult will it be to move out?*
   a. The Britney Spears dolls alone will take weeks to
      catalog. (+5)
   b. I'll probably do one lap with a leaf blower to get
      everything organized. (+3)
   c. Goodwill, here I come! (-1)
   d. No problem. I have the moving company's phone
      number on my speed dial. (-5)

14. Do you have any pets (or anything else) buried in the backyard? (+5)

15. Were any parts of the house hand-built by you or anyone close to you? (+5)

Here's how the scores break down:

150–170: You probably require an intervention and/or
   professional counseling.
120–150: You've got some work to do. Remember, it's just a
   house, and you'll love your new place just as much.
90–120: You should be able to make a clean break pretty easily.
65–90: You're ready to go. Take the first halfway decent offer
   and run!

MAKE A CLEAN BREAK

Now that you know just how attached you are to your house, here are a few suggestions to help you disconnect from it. We know it's difficult, but in the end it will be worth it.

1. *Depersonalize.* Your house is filled with emotional triggers, from wedding photos to the kids' height chart on the kitchen wall. The sooner you can remove those things from sight, the easier the transition will be.

2. *Crunch the numbers.* As you know by now, you need to start thinking of your home as a commodity. To do this, start thinking of its value more in terms of the sale price you'll get for it and less about its

You *Can* Take It With You

Regardless of how attached you may be to your house, there may be a few items that would otherwise be sold with the house that you would like to take with you when you leave. Buyers expect certain items, like built-in appliances and light fixtures, to be included in the purchase price. If you want to keep any of these items, you'll be better off removing and replacing them *before* you put your house on the market, rather than disclosing to the buyers afterward that you'll be taking those items. That way it won't even arise as an issue, and letting you take those things won't seem like a concession from the buyers (for which they'll definitely want something in return).

personal and emotional value. Use www.zillow.com or another home valuation site to keep track of your home's value and also to keep an eye on comparable local sales.

3. *Get nostalgic.* Think back to when you first bought your house. We'll bet you had big plans for all the wonderful things you would do in the house. You might have imagined sipping champagne in a hammock out back, or having a huge Super Bowl party in the TV room. If you haven't done any of those things yet, do them before you move out. They may provide a sense of closure for you.

4. *Party!* If all else fails, throw yourself a huge moving-out party. Remember, you should start moving out the moment you decide to sell, so don't wait to throw the party. Once the party's over, it'll be easier to think of the house as no longer really yours.

WHAT'S YOUR SCHEDULE?

It's said that time is money, and there are few endeavors when that is more true than selling your home. Every extra day before you close is another day that you'll incur carrying costs such as mortgage interest, utilities, taxes, and insurance (see "Buzzword: Carrying Costs" in Step 2). And if you need to coordinate between selling your current home and buying your new one, any scheduling problems can cost thousands of dollars. We've talked about how important it is to set a goal of selling as quickly as possible, and figuring out the best schedule for yourself can go a long way toward meeting that goal. The best way to do that is to complete a time line of the entire process.

To complete your time line, start by entering the date you want to close the sale and be completely moved out. Then work back in time from there to determine the approximate dates that you'll need to get everything else done along the way. Keep in mind, if you're also buying a new home simultaneously, the process can get much more complicated. Be sure to consider the buying schedule when determining your seller's time line. Finally, if you fill out the "Seller's Time Line" table below and realize that the starting date has long since passed, you've got some work to do. Meet with your agent immediately to figure out the best way to get you out the door in time.

SELLER'S TIME LINE

What You're Doing	Sample Dates	Your Dates
Close and move out	August 31	
Start packing	**GO BACK 1 MONTH TO** July 31 (assuming one month to pack everything)	
Accept offer	**GO BACK 2 WEEKS TO** July 15 (or local days on the market)	
House goes on the market	**GO BACK 1 MONTH TO** June 15	
Finish staging	**GO BACK 1 WEEK TO** June 8	
1. Begin cleaning (or hire cleaning crew) 2. Begin interior staging	**GO BACK 1 WEEK TO** June 1	
1. Choose agent 2. Fertilize/replant 3. Start packing personal items	**GO BACK 1 MONTH TO** May 1	
1. Start interviewing agents	**GO BACK TWO WEEKS TO** April 15	
1. Start going to open houses 2. Visit model homes	**GO BACK TWO WEEKS TO** April 1	

As you can see, this is a long process and there's a lot to do. Setting a schedule and doing your best to stick to it can go a long way toward ensuring a successful sale.

Other Important Events to Schedule

If you're doing any significant remodeling or repairs, you obviously want to start as early as possible, to make sure the inevitable delays don't keep you from listing your house on schedule. As a rule of thumb, you should assume that any job will take twice as long (and probably cost twice as much) as your contractor estimates.

As we mentioned earlier, if you're going to have a prelisting home inspection done, schedule it before any remodeling and/or repairs. That way you can fix any defects the inspector finds while you're having the other work done.

You could schedule your farewell party either well in advance of listing the house, to begin distancing yourself emotionally, or you could wait until the last minute when everything is pretty much moved out. Just remember that you are obligated to deliver the house to the sellers in the same condition as when they submitted their offer. Unfortunately, that means you will have to clean up after everyone leaves.

WHAT KIND OF CLIENT WILL YOU BE?

In Step 2 we'll figure out how to find the perfect real estate agent for you. Before we can do that, we need to determine what kind of client you'll be, so you can then find somebody with whom you can work most honestly and efficiently. There are as many different types of sellers as there are sellers themselves. They all bring their own personalities to bear on the selling process. Knowing who you are and how you'll engage with the process can help you avoid conflicts, frustrations, and disappointments down the road.

If you decide to go the for-sale-by-owner route, you'll need to be particularly honest with yourself here. Are you ready to oversee every detail throughout the process, and are you self-motivated enough to do all that it'll take to make going FSBO worthwhile? Since you'll be playing both roles and won't have the benefit of an objective outside opinion throughout the process, make sure you don't let your ego get in the way of making informed, unemotional decisions. That's not to suggest that FSBOs have bigger egos than other sellers, just that good agents are skilled in the art of keeping their clients' egos in check throughout the process.

Hands On or Off?

The first question to ask yourself is, Are you the type of seller who wants to be hands on or hands off? Will you be comfortable trusting your agent to handle everything for you and just get you involved when you need to be? Or will you lie awake at night worrying about every little detail? Most likely, you're somewhere in the middle, but regardless it's important to know ahead of time.

Hands-on Sellers   If you're the hands-on type, you need to find an agent who is receptive to that style of client. Otherwise, she might get frustrated with you and end up doing you a disservice. The default mode for most good agents that we know is to protect their clients by limiting their exposure to the nitty-gritty details. Some clients interpret that to mean their agents are hiding things from them. The reality is that style allows the agents to do the best job for their clients. That's not to say you should change your style, but just make sure the agent you pick knows going in that you want to be involved and is okay with it. You should expect a lot of communication with your agent and she should be willing to run everything by you before making decisions. You need to be willing to have your agent disagree with you and tell you exactly why. If you have opinions on everything, you could share them, but understand that your agent probably has much more experience with selling homes than you do. You don't need to defer to your agent on every little thing, but you also don't want to make decisions based on pride rather than experience. And you definitely don't want to push your agent out to the periphery of the transaction. A good agent needs to understand the big picture and pull everything together properly.

Basically, we find that overly involved clients tend to make many of the same mistakes that FSBOs do. They often reveal too much to prospective buyers, they schedule too many open houses (thereby overexposing the house), they can easily appear desperate, and they negotiate poorly. In the end, a good agent can't do her job, and it's the seller who ultimately suffers.

Hands-off Sellers   If you're the hands-off type, you may just want to sign the listing agreement and show up for the closing but otherwise stay out of the loop. Unfortunately, that's not a realistic approach. Legally, you have to disclose any problems with the house to the buyer. Some problems—like a worn-out roof or a leaky pipe—might be obvious to the most casual visitor. There might be other problems that are more difficult to detect, anything from springtime flooding to a prior death in the house (yes, you may actually need to disclose that). Your agent won't know about these issues unless you tell him or her about them. And guess what? You can't plead ignorance after the fact. So you need to do your due diligence and put in the time to complete the required disclosures for the buyer.

Another problem with a completely hands-off approach is that if you suddenly want to get involved late in the game, it's much more difficult if you haven't kept up with the progress of the sale.

* * *

OUR best clients are moderately hands on. If you're the type to end up on either extreme, try to bring yourself back toward the middle. Extremely hands-on sellers need to pull back a bit and allow their agents to work for them. Extremely hands-off sellers need to get a bit more involved in the process.

How Motivated Are You?

It's not that we expect clients to work full time on selling their homes, but if they're driven to succeed they'll find a way to make sure everything gets done. We also find that motivated clients make us better agents, since we can work together closely and bring lots of good ideas and energy to the process.

C'mon, be honest: Are you really ready to do *everything* possible to have a truly successful sale? Are you willing to keep your home spotless every day it might be shown? Are you willing to spend the money up front to stage your house properly to attract the best-qualified buyers? It's okay to admit that you're not. But if you are, your agent will really enjoy working with you, and you'll get your money's worth from her commission. Additionally, this kind of motivation shows that you're a serious seller, so your agent will be comfortable talking openly and honestly with you. As we'll see in Step 2, that's really the foundation of a good working relationship and, consequently, a successful sale.

Do You Know What You Don't Know?

Both extremely hands-on sellers and FSBOs are susceptible to thinking they know everything they need to know. As Socrates said, "The only true wisdom is in knowing you know nothing." Actually, that may be a bit extreme, but we certainly agree that the opposite is true: it is supremely unwise to think you know everything.

We'll say this again and again: the biggest risk of selling without an agent is not just that you can't know everything you need to know (we've been in this business full time for a long time and we learn something new every day), you also probably don't know what you don't know, which in a financial transaction as significant as selling your house can have devastating consequences.

Here's a perfect example: Steve and Amanda owned their house for about ten years. When they bought it, the listing said there were hardwood floors throughout. Shortly after they moved in, they went to have the floors refinished and found out that they were, in fact, just wood laminate. They were surprised but figured they'd learned a valuable lesson and didn't do anything about it (although they could have sued to have real wood floors installed). When they got ready to sell, they considered going FSBO, but they also talked to us. They wanted to include the "hardwood floors" in the listing. They were surprised when we told them they'd just be asking for a lawsuit. The point is, our society is much more litigious now than it was ten years ago. Things change so quickly that a real estate experience of even just a few years ago can be seriously outdated.

INSIDER SECRET

2

Find Your SOLDmate

WE DON'T EXPECT you to instantly trust our sincerity when we tell you how important a real estate agent is to successful selling, so here's our best effort to convince you: We really, really, *really* believe that a good agent is essential to successful selling. If you could see us now, you'd see that we're pleading with you, with expressions of genuine support and a sympathetic hand on your shoulder. And we're not just saying this because we've made a good living helping our clients sell their homes but because we've seen what can happen to sellers who hire the wrong agents or who decide to sell their homes themselves. *In fact, if we were selling our own houses, we wouldn't go it alone.* Even with all of our expertise in real estate, we need the buffer and objectivity that a good agent provides to keep us relatively sane throughout the process.

It's hard to overestimate the value of the objective advice and unemotional guidance you gain from hiring a good agent. A solid working relationship with that agent greatly increases your

Do Agents Actually Earn Their Money?

The most recent "Profile of Home Buyers and Sellers" released by the National Association of Realtors (NAR) found that in 2005 the median sale price for a home sold with an agent was 16 percent higher than the sale price for homes sold without an agent. Now, you have every right to be skeptical, given that the NAR itself clearly benefits from the result. While the study was careful to compare similar houses, it is possible that FSBOs are systematically more likely to appear in lower-priced markets. So let's assume that the NAR's conclusion is wildly optimistic. Suppose it overestimated the effect of agents by more than 200 percent and that the difference was not 16 percent but actually only 5.1%, which was the average commission rate in 2004, according to *Real Trends* magazine. If that were the case, then sellers who used agents would pocket the same amount of money as those who sold themselves. Along the way, though, represented sellers would have done much less work, experienced much less stress, and incurred much less liability. So the basic question is, If you were going to end up with the same amount of money anyway (or probably even more), why wouldn't you go with an agent?

chances of getting the best price in the shortest time and avoiding any troublesome issues (and lawsuits!). Plus, we can't ignore the wisdom of Abraham Lincoln, who said, "He who represents himself has a fool for a client."

THE CASE FOR AGENTS

We understand what motivates people to sell their homes themselves, and we can see how it may seem attractive. Folks who go the FSBO route just seem to have a different way of thinking. "Selling real estate isn't rocket science," they say, "so why should I give up 5 percent or 6 percent to someone who's just going to unlock the door for the showings and shuffle some papers at the closing?"

Let us show you why we believe you should use an agent.

A Good Agent Follows All the Steps to Get You the Best Price

The marketplace sets the price for a house. After all, what else could determine the true value of a home other than what a real buyer is willing and able to pay for it, and what a credible bank is willing to lend? Our experience has shown that it's very difficult to get more than the market value for your home but all too easy to get a whole lot less. The expertise and experience that your agent provides will help you do *everything* right to make sure you don't leave any money on the table, including:

- Honestly and unemotionally discuss necessary improvements and repairs.

- Help you set the proper listing price.

- "Stage" your house inside and out—or arrange for an expert to do it—to make it as appealing to buyers as possible.

- List your house with the Multiple Listing Service (MLS), *the* source that buyers' agents use to find properties for their clients.

- Arrange brokers' open houses and caravans, as well as networking through office meetings to attract agents representing serious buyers.

- Market your home through newspaper ads, online listings, and signage with a direct phone number.

- Coordinate showings and provide a lockbox for security.

Realtor® Versus Real Estate Agent

Clients constantly ask us about this distinction, and also what's the deal with the ® symbol? It's actually very simple. *Agent* is a generic term that refers to any number of different jobs in the real estate business. The term *Realtor®* can only be used by members of the National Association of Realtors®. Those members voluntarily hold themselves to a strict code of ethics established by the NAR, designed to protect consumers and establish greater professional credibility within the industry. And, by the way, that little ® symbol just means that the term *"Realtor®"* is a registered trademark, so it can't be used by anyone but NAR members.

While you may certainly find an excellent agent who is not an NAR member, we believe that membership does indicate a certain dedication to the profession and an acknowledgment that professional standards should be achieved by everyone in the field. Therefore, you shouldn't ignore the term *Realtor®* as just a marketing gimmick; it does represent something important to you in your quest for a successful sale. So, if you're interviewing an agent who is not a *Realtor®*, you may want to ask them about it.

Of course, throughout this book you'll see us use the term *agent* rather than *Realtor®*. That's just because we want to speak to every seller along the way, regardless of whether or not his or her real estate agent is a member of the NAR. Plus, having that ® show up everywhere throughout the book would get really annoying.

BUZZWORD

- Provide a network of local, trustworthy tradespeople and professionals, such as plumbers, electricians, and carpenters, as well as a team of support staff who all have a different role in the sale of your home (title, escrow, home warranty, appraiser, etc.).

- Review offers and determine which are truly the best—not always the highest—to make sure you don't lose a buyer, take your home off the market, and go back to square one.

A Good Agent Knows Your Neighborhood and Understands What Works to Get the Most Value Out of Your House

Dedicated agents know all the relevant information about their territories, including detailed data about recent sales (condition, improvements, how it was staged, etc.), information about schools, and even what the local city council has on its agenda. For example, we were recently referred to a neighbor of a client in the same development. We knew everything about that area, from the different floor plans of the houses to the SAT scores of the local high school students. Our original client had put in hardwood floors and upgraded the master bath, so we knew exactly how prospective buyers responded to those improvements.

The neighbor needed to sell quickly but also needed to get a good price. We were able to accurately price his home immediately, refer contractors to get some repairs done in just a few days, and deliver the same team to handle the details that we'd worked with for the original client. Our intimate knowledge of his home and neighborhood allowed him to get a great price for the house and to do so very quickly, ultimately saving him from leaving thousands of dollars behind.

A Good Agent Helps You Navigate the Process and Keeps You Out of Court

What most sellers don't consider is how important an agent can be in ensuring that your transaction doesn't become a legal nightmare. We often tell sellers considering FSBO that if there's going to be a future get-together with the buyers, they want it to be in the living room, not the courtroom. As much as we respect the FSBO's entrepreneurial spirit (after all, that same spirit is what got us into this business in the first place), we know how risky it is to embark on a financial venture without extensive knowledge and experience. From disclosures to financing, from tax laws to negotiations, we've learned through experience how complex modern real estate transactions have become.

You certainly wouldn't trust something as important as your health to anyone other than a qualified physician, and you shouldn't trust your most significant financial transaction to anyone other than a qualified real estate agent. As we mentioned before, we often tell people considering going FSBO that the biggest risk is that they "don't know what they don't know." In this day and age, that's a scary prospect indeed. Even the smallest oversight can result in a lawsuit and a huge financial loss for sellers. Here's just a tiny sample of the types of disclosure issues that potentially could get sellers into real trouble:

Are You Selling a House of Death?   Believe it or not, some states require that sellers disclose deaths that have taken place in the house. We have represented sellers who were heirs to a relative who died in the home. They were amazed to find out that the death needed to be disclosed to potential buyers.

Electrical Field Shocks Buyer   Not only are sellers required to disclose everything they know about the house, they're also required to alert buyers of their rights to investigate any number of unknown potential problems. We represented a buyer who insisted on conducting an electrical field survey of the power lines behind the house. The agent representing the seller was surprised that this type of inspection was even an option for a buyer.

Size Matters   The square footage you present in your disclosure must be accurate. We've seen buyers discover a discrepancy between what was represented to them by the seller and the actual area. In one case they sued to recover several hundred dollars per square foot of the difference. It's essential that sellers use the

Disclosure Statement

Years ago, it was "buyer beware" in the real estate business, but now sellers are obligated to disclose just about everything about their house to a potential buyer. In fact, keeping up-to-date with all of the local disclosure requirements is one of the more daunting challenges facing a good agent. As we'll see in Step 3, it's actually in your best interest to provide as much information as possible to a buyer. You may think that what they don't know can't hurt them, but in fact what they don't know can hurt *you*. They're going to find everything out eventually, and you could either end up with a canceled sale or, worse, a lawsuit.

We sit down with every client and carefully complete several disclosure statements. The statements require the seller to reveal all the relevant features of their home, as well as past and/or current issues such as mold, asbestos, lead paint, insurance claims, and even noise nuisances. For example, sellers must disclose to buyers that the neighbors' kids have a band and they practice every night in the garage next door. But the disclosures don't stop there. As we noted above, the seller is also legally obligated to allow the buyer to check for issues the seller may not know about through any number of different inspections. In this case, ignorance is definitely *not* an excuse.

The entire disclosure process is set up to protect the buyers from unknown problems, and they hold all the cards. In other words, you won't be able to hide anything from them. So your best bet is to complete as many repairs and renovations as necessary before putting the house on the market (see Step 4), disclose everything that's still an issue, and allow and encourage the buyers to look into any other issues they're worried about.

BUZZWORD

proper forms and language to make sure they're protected from just such a problem.

Sprinkler System Could Leave Seller All Wet We sat down recently to fill out a disclosure statement with a couple whose house we were just about to list. The husband completed the form, noting all the features and issues that the house had. We all noticed, his wife included, when he checked the box indicating they had an automatic lawn sprinkler system. We three ladies shot glances to each other around the table, and we suggested he uncheck that box. We all knew that, in fact, his "system" consisted of a spigot, a hose, and one of those wavy sprinklers we used to play in when we were kids. And the only time it was "automatic" was when someone else turned on the hose for him.

These and countless other required disclosures could easily become major issues for a seller. Suppose we didn't catch that sprinkler disclosure? He would have closed on the house, the buyers would have discovered the discrepancy, and they could have sued to have a real automatic sprinkler system installed to the tune of several thousand dollars.

A good agent's thorough understanding of the many legal issues that can arise helps sellers steer clear of any costly pitfalls.

SO, YOU'RE STILL GOING FSBO?

We hope that the tangible (higher prices and fewer lawsuits) and intangible (less stress and uncertainty) advantages of using an agent will relieve any doubts that a good agent is worth his or her commission, but we know some people are committed to selling themselves, and we wish them the best of luck. If that's the case, though, we have a few additional pieces of advice.

First of all, you need to hire a good real estate attorney. In some parts of the country lawyers are required at certain points in the process, but even if it's not required, a lawyer should review your disclosures, offers, and other pertinent paperwork. Keep in mind that a lawyer is not a substitute for an agent, since he won't have the intimate knowledge of your neighborhood or house. Even with a lawyer, you may still run into the same disclosure problems we talked about earlier because it's such a complex process and it's simply not in a lawyer's job description to get

involved in all the details. (You can find a lawyer at www
.RealEstateLawyers.com, which also has a lot of additional information on the legal aspects of real estate transactions.)

Second, be sure to read this book very carefully and heed all
the insider advice we provide. We can't say enough that one of the
most important things all sellers must do is "cut the cord"—
distance themselves emotionally from the entire process. Most
people find this very difficult to do, but it's essential to successful
selling. Since you won't have an agent to present an objective
viewpoint, be sure to find someone who won't just tell you what
you want to hear but who will tell the truth about your house and
your best course of action.

There are lots of other risks involved in a FSBO transaction.
Many may be overcome if you do your homework, but others
you'll simply have to deal with and take your chances. Here are a
few issues to keep in mind:

What's Wrong with This Ad?

It might seem like writing a real estate ad is a simple process, but this basic task can
present serious problems for sellers who are unfamiliar with the law. Take a look at
this seemingly innocuous ad and see if you can spot the lawsuits waiting to happen:

**Totally remodeled 4-bedroom home perfect for a growing family! Good family
neighborhood, safe street, within walking distance to church and school, gigantic
yard great for kids. Sparkling new appliances throughout the gourmet kitchen.
Spacious bath with Jacuzzi tub. 2,497 square feet of new living space with unlimited
possibilities for expansion.**

Did you find all ten—that's right, ten!—potential problems? Let's see what they are.

1. *You can't say "totally remodeled," since nothing is ever* totally *remodeled. Were
the walls torn down to the studs? Was all the plumbing replaced? Electrical? Or
was it just a cosmetic improvement?*

continued

2. You can't say "growing family," since it shows a possible bias for the type of family the sellers are looking for. If a childless couple has their offer rejected, they can claim they were discriminated against.

3. You can't say "good neighborhood/safe street," since it implies that the seller is guaranteeing a safety issue. What if there is ever a crime? Will the seller be seen to have misrepresented the reality of the neighborhood?

4. You can't say "walking distance," since it assumes that all buyers will be able to walk comfortably the same distance. What if a person in a wheelchair has their offer rejected?

5. You can't say "church and school," since it shows a potential bias toward buyers with kids as well as those of certain religious beliefs.

6. You can't say "gigantic yard for kids," since one person's idea of gigantic is different from another's. In addition, a "kids'" yard shows bias.

7. You can't say "new appliances" unless they have never been used.

8. You can only use brand names (like Jacuzzi or Corian) if the items are of that exact brand.

9. You shouldn't say "2,497 square feet," since quoting an exact square footage puts you at risk. The house could easily be measured differently by an appraiser.

10. You shouldn't say "unlimited possibilities for expansion," since that implies a guarantee that the buyers will be able to build their dream home with no thought to the local building restrictions.

This may seem like nitpicking, and that's exactly our point. It's our job as agents to make sure all the little details are accounted for. You may laugh at how ridiculous some of these "violations" may be, but we can guarantee that you won't be laughing when the judge finds in favor of the plaintiff and you owe damages for discrimination.

Here's how the ad should read:

Updated 4-bedroom home perfect for those in need of plenty of square footage! Highly desirable neighborhood, tree-lined street, located in an award-winning school district. Oversized yard great for entertaining and enjoying the mountain views. Newer appliances throughout the gourmet kitchen. Approx. 2,497 square feet of living space (buyer to verify size) with a possibility of further expansion.

You May Not Be Able to List with the Multiple Listing Service

Real estate agents use the MLS as their primary means of gathering information about homes on the market. Getting your house listed in the MLS is a huge part of selling successfully. The MLS is starting to open up to nonagents, but it's still a restricted source of information. Moreover, when buyers' agents see that your house is a FSBO listing, they're likely to steer clear to avoid the potential hassles of dealing directly with a seller. You may be perfectly qualified to sell your house, but you just won't attract the quantity (or quality) of buyers that you'd get with an agent. We know it sounds unfair, but that's the way it is.

Buyers Will Be Bargain Hunters

Every buyer wants to find a good deal, but most of the buyers attracted to FSBO listings are serious bargain hunters who figure there will be less competition for the house and that they will be able to haggle you down to the rock-bottom price. When *you* see a FSBO sign out in front of a house, what's the first thought that pops into *your* mind? For us, it's just one word: bargain. That is exactly the wrong mind-set you want buyers to have when they visit your house.

Most FSBO sellers, though, assume they'll get market price for their house, and many believe they can do even better. So right off the bat the buyers and sellers are very far apart on the price.

Combine all this with the likelihood that many buyers interested in FSBO properties don't work with agents (they're usually driving around, see the sign, and call you directly), and you've got a recipe for disaster.

Your House Is Open to the Public

You might find it hard to believe that strangers would knock on your door early Sunday morning, greeting you in all your bathrobed and bed-headed glory, but we can guarantee they will.

The Evolution of Agents

People ask us all the time if real estate agents are about to go the way of the dinosaurs. Especially with the Internet providing so much information to sellers, aren't agents becoming unnecessary? We don't see agents disappearing anytime soon, but our role will most definitely evolve in the coming years. And that's a good thing for everyone. While real estate markets will always heat up and cool down, one thing will remain certain: real estate agents will possess *some* amount of expertise that our clients will find valuable enough to pay for. The important questions are, How much of that expertise can sellers track down themselves, and how independent of agents can sellers become and still ensure a safe and successful sale? Right now, the answer to both questions is "not much," but that's changing.

There are already thousands of Web sites that provide information for sellers (some of which we recommend in the Resources section of this book). As these sites, and the sellers who use them, get more sophisticated, real estate agents will need to change the way we do business. For example, there are already several sites that provide excellent information on setting listing prices like HomeSmartReports.com, which offers a "HomeSmart Value Report," utilizing the same methods that mortgage lenders use. Also, the Internet is slowly but surely eroding the exclusivity of the MLS. As the MLS becomes more accessible, and eventually may become open to the public, real estate agents will become somewhat less valuable (which is borne out by the fact that average commissions have decreased from right around 6 percent to 5.1 percent in recent years). But extinct? We don't think so.

Good agents will always command a fair price for their expertise and knowledge of local laws, regulations, and market details—not to mention an objective appraisal of your home's appeal. Frankly, we look forward to the changes. When sellers are better informed, diligent, and professional, agents can focus on what we do best. Unprofessional agents will fall by the wayside, leaving the industry stronger and leaving us more able to focus on the needs of our clients.

Because they're bargain hunters and because you won't have an agent as an intermediary, all sense of privacy tends to fly out the window once you go FSBO. With an agent, nobody gets in the house who isn't qualified and accompanied by their agent. Plus, agents will provide the added protection of a lockbox, which digitally records who is accessing your home and when. As a FSBO, you really have no idea who is coming to your house and little ability to regulate when they stop by. We're not trying to scare you into hiring an agent; we're just trying to inform you about *all* of the valuable services that an agent provides for his or her commission. If you're set on going FSBO, skip ahead to Step 3. But if you're reconsidering finding a real estate agent, read on.

HOW TO FIND A GREAT AGENT

We know . . . it seems like everyone and his mother is "in real estate" these days, so it can be a daunting task to find the right person to work with. We want sellers to be true partners with their agents. We've had the most success when sellers are educated about the process and work together with us to make the best deal happen. So how can you find a real estate agent who will work as hard for his or her clients as we do? Here are three strategies to help you narrow your search and find two or three agents to consider seriously:

Referrals

As with so many things, word of mouth is by far the best way to find a good real estate agent. Talk to your friends and neighbors who have bought or sold recently. Ask them if they were satisfied with the agent and the overall experience. Also, ask if there was anything they *didn't* like about their agent.

Keep in mind that one of the best compliments an agent can get may not sound exactly positive. We love it when clients tell us how happy they are with the outcome but then chide us for not having to work too hard for our commission. "Maybe the next sale will be tougher," they say. We love this, because it means we've done our job and successfully kept the seller away from all the aggravation and complexity of the process. So if a friend tells you she made a killing on her house, and her agent sold it without breaking a sweat, that's probably a great referral.

Open Houses

Go to a few open houses in your neighborhood and see if you like any of the agents. This is a good opportunity to see agents in action. Do they look and act professional? Do they answer questions clearly and confidently? Imagine that this was your house being sold. Would you be happy with how you are being represented?

Mailings

Nobody likes to get junk mail, but in this case it might actually be helpful. Agents who send out postcards of recent sales or other local information (we call it "farming") tend to have excellent knowledge of your neighborhood and are probably serious about their business. We'd never suggest that you only talk to agents from these mailings, but it would be worth contacting one or two. Your best bet is to contact those agents whose mailings you've consistently received over a long period of time.

TOP TEN QUESTIONS TO ASK PROSPECTIVE AGENTS

Okay, you've found a couple of candidates. Now how do you find out which one to list with? You'll want to interview each one to get a better sense of his or her experience and approach to the sales process. Keep in mind that you're the boss here, so it's most important that you feel comfortable with this person representing you. But also remember that you're relying on this person's expertise to have a successful sale, so listen carefully to how your questions are answered.

1. What's your experience in the business? Ideally, you're looking for someone with experience in your area and who is clearly professional and dedicated. Don't necessarily go just by years of experience. Newer agents may actually know the market well and understand the current laws, while veterans may be less dedicated and up-to-date.

Red flag: Definitely look out for anyone who only does real estate part time. This is a complicated business, and you want to hire a full-time professional dedicated to your cause.

2. How many agents are in your office? Is there a receptionist? These questions are intended to help you determine if this agent has the necessary business functions in place to sell your house. You don't necessarily need an agent who is part of a large agency, but you do want to know that they network with other agents in the area. Asking about a receptionist may seem like an insignificant question, but the answer can speak volumes about this agent's professionalism. Interested buyers must be able to speak to a real, live person when they call about a listing. If there's no receptionist, good brokers will make sure that all calls are forwarded to their cell phones.

Part-Timer Trouble

When we work with buyers, we often encounter sellers who have fallen into many of the traps we talk about throughout this book. One of the most painful to watch was a seller whose agent worked only part time in real estate. The buyer was referred to us by a satisfied former client (we love when that happens!) and needed to buy a home immediately because of a job transfer. We'd heard of a place that had just gone on the market. The buyers liked the house and were prepared to make a full-price offer. Unfortunately, the seller's agent was out of town for his real job and was unreachable. The buyers had no choice but to pull their offer and find another place.

FOOL'S FABLE

One factor that may lead you toward a larger agency is to lower your risk of lawsuit, if somewhat indirectly. Any serious agency will carry errors and omissions (E&O) insurance, which will cover agents in case they get sued. Larger agencies, which are assumed to have deeper pockets (more to sue for), will have more coverage and therefore higher premiums. These agencies can lower their premiums through professional education programs to keep their agents up-to-date on the latest laws and regulations. Obviously, a better-educated agent is more likely to keep you out of trouble. By the way, the agent's E&O insurance does not necessarily protect his or her client, who is also likely to get caught up in the lawsuit, so you'll want to do everything you can to stay out of court in the first place.

Red flag: Independent agents can do a great job, but they need to have their business set up properly. Interested buyers need to get a real person on the phone if they want information on a property; much of the time they won't leave messages. Agents who are not aware of this are probably missing many other important strategies as well.

3. *How will you market and advertise my house?* You want an agent who understands that the more potential qualified buyers you attract, the better you'll do. Your agent should plan a brokers' open house, which is much more important to you than regular open houses. (If he holds open houses, keep in mind that he's probably doing so to get more clients for himself rather than exclusively to sell your house.) Good agents will also advertise in local newspapers, Web sites, and with a yard sign. They'll take several photos of your house, print up professional flyers, and arrange for an online virtual tour. Finally, they should arrange to have a lockbox at your house to allow agents to bring their qualified clients by for scheduled showings. Ask to see sample promotional materials from other properties to get a sense of their style.

Be sure to keep a written record of everything the agent proposes to do to sell your house. A good agent will likely keep an "activity list" himself to record everything he's done, and at some point down the road you may want to make sure that he did everything he said he was going to do.

Red flag: If any agents tell you that they've already got a buyer lined up for your house, you should be very wary. This type of agent is playing on your emotions and trying to hook you in with the prospect of a quick sale. Successful selling is hard work, and anyone who claims to have a shortcut is probably not looking out for your best interests. Also, beware agents who don't want to list on the MLS right away. They're probably trying to find a buyer from an agent within their office and once again are most interested in their commission rather than your interests.

4. *What are some other comparable recent sales in the area?* Good agents should know about all the recent sales and current listings in your area and ideally will have sold some comparable properties themselves.

Open Houses Don't Sell Homes

Most sellers believe that open houses are invaluable when their house is on the market. After all, there's lots of activity, often with dozens of seemingly enthusiastic buyers stopping by to check out your place. The problem is that open houses are much more about quantity than quality. The vast majority of people visiting an open house are "tire kickers," just taking a casual tour to see what's out there, or neighbors curious to see the place on the inside. They're very rarely serious buyers. We also see lots of people who just can't afford the house and want to spend their Sunday on a neighborhood home tour.

In fact, of the hundreds of houses we've sold over the years, we can count on one hand the number that sold off an open house.

What will sell houses are brokers' open houses, sometimes called caravans, in which lots of local brokers will stop by without their clients and check out a new listing. This is how agents generate buzz about a house. After the caravan, the agents will contact all of their clients who they think would be interested in the house. So a single caravan is likely to generate real interest from several serious buyers.

INSIDER SECRET

They should mention that they provide a competitive market analysis (CMA) to their clients (see "Buzzword: Competitive Market Analysis" opposite). Before we meet with prospective clients, we always make sure we're current on the local scene (most of the time we already know what's going on, but we check out the MLS and talk to other agents to make sure). It's the least we can do to show someone we want their business.

Red flag: If an agent can't rattle off several recent local sales and tell you the listing/sale price, the market time, and the general condition of the home, he either doesn't know your neighborhood very well or he wasn't enthusiastic enough about your interview to do a little research. Either way, this is probably not someone who is going to provide you with the best service.

5. *Do you offer a staging service?* You want an agent who understands the importance of staging and will help you get your house ready to show. We'll explore staging in detail in Step 5, but for now just realize that staging is intended to show your house in the best possible light and generate enthusiasm from other agents and serious buyers. Your agent should schedule a walk-through and understand exactly how to accentuate the best features of your house (and to downplay its less appealing parts).

Red flag: If they give you a blank stare that tells you they've never heard the term *staging* before, that's a problem. If they tell you that they don't think it's necessary in your area, that's also a problem.

6. *What is a good listing price for my house?* Listing prices should be based on the *sales price* of comparable homes that have recently sold. Don't look at listings currently on the market, since listing prices can vary wildly. It's only the sales price that matters. After all, if appraisers primarily use sold prices to set their values, then sellers should as well. Ask the agent to give you sale prices for several comparable homes

that sold recently. For a more detailed analysis of how to set a listing price, see "Setting the Listing Price" on page 73.

Red flag: This one is similar to the agent who has a buyer already lined up. Beware agents with estimates that appear too good to be true (because they probably are). If your neighbor's comparable house just sold for $300,000 and an agent says yours could easily get $400,000, they're more than likely not being realistic. Remember, you need an agent who will be brutally honest with you, not someone who just tells you what you want to hear.

Competitive Market Analysis

As you interview possible agents, they should provide you with a competitive market analysis—also known as a comparative market analysis—for your house, which will be particularly useful when it comes to setting your listing price. A CMA is simply a summary of all the local activity on houses similar to yours. Most CMAs will include active listings (homes currently on the market), listings under agreement, and recently sold homes (usually within the last six months). *Remember, for purposes of setting your listing price, only closed sales are relevant.* You simply cannot assume that the listings under agreement are done deals or that the homes on the market are priced properly.

You can also use the CMA to determine which agent is best for you. Some agents might include properties in a CMA that don't belong there, to give prospective clients a sense that their homes are worth more than they actually are. Look carefully at the listings included in a CMA and make sure that they actually are comparable to your home. Check the number of bedrooms and bathrooms, the square footage, and the year the house was built. And since you're probably familiar with your local neighborhoods, also note if the houses on the CMA are in pricier areas than your own. As much as you would like to believe that your house is worth more than it actually is, try to be completely honest with yourself since the consequences of listing your house too high can be serious.

BUZZWORD

7. What is a good sale price for my home? We believe that homes should sell for pretty close to their listing price. We don't believe that listing prices affect sale prices very much (as we said before, only the market can actually determine the sale price). So a good agent should tell you that they expect your home to sell for pretty close to what it's listed for. If they start pitching the idea of sparking a bidding war (which does sometimes happen, but shouldn't be assumed), you should be wary.

Red flag: As we've seen, some agents tell you what you want to hear to get your listing, rather than leveling with you. Agents who suggest your house will sell for well above asking price are just buttering you up.

8. What happens if you represent a potential buyer? You want an agent who's exclusively working for you, representing your interests as a seller. Selling your house can have major financial and legal consequences, and your agent must appreciate that. The only answers you want to hear are either (1) "I don't 'double-pop' (represent both sides), so it won't be a problem" or (2) "If that comes up, I will refer the buyer to another agent. After all, I work for you."

You also want to be sure that your agent's office doesn't offer any incentives to keep sales in-house. Since agencies double their earnings if both the buyer's and seller's agents come from their office, they may offer a bonus to the agents if this is the case. We even know of some agencies that keep new listings off the broader market for a few weeks to try and find a buyer in-house. This arrangement obviously limits your pool of potential buyers and represents a significant potential conflict of interest.

Red flag: This is a really tricky issue, and one that good real estate agents know how to handle. Here's what you don't want to hear: "Well, if that happens I'll reduce my commission. How's that for a great deal?" Well, it's *potentially* a great deal, but it's more than likely a lousy deal. Sure, you might save a little money, but you're giving up independent representation in a huge financial transaction. If you were being sued, would you feel all right if your lawyer suggested that he'd cut his fee because he was also representing the other side? Of course you wouldn't. And you shouldn't give up your real estate agent's complete representation for any price. It's just too risky.

9. *What will the duration of our listing agreement be? Do you offer an "opt-out" clause?* A good agent should reference recent sales and the average days on market (DOM) for your area and offer to list for about a month beyond that. Also, agents shouldn't balk at your request for an "opt-out" clause, allowing you to terminate your listing if you're dissatisfied with their work. Ideally, they should offer to add it.

Red flag: Agents will obviously want you to commit to them for as long a time as possible, but it's in your best interest not to be locked in for too long. When agents show you comparable homes that have sold recently, ask about the DOM figures (you'll find the number somewhere on an MLS listing sheet) to get a sense of how hot the market is. You'll want your listing period to be a few weeks longer than the average DOM. If an agent is pushing for a much longer period (for example, six months in a hot market is way too long), they're not being straight with you.

10. *What do I need to do to prepare my house for the market?* Experienced agents will know exactly what to do (and what not to do) to get your house ready for sale. We'll talk about many of these things in Steps 4 and 5. He or she should understand that how you live in your home and how you sell it are two very different things. You have to think like a businessperson selling a commodity, regardless of how personally attached you are to it. Generally, your agent should suggest that as many repairs as possible are made, the house is spotlessly cleaned, and that it is properly staged for showing. If they have not done so already, the agent should schedule a walk-through and work closely with you to make sure everything is done properly.

Red flag: Getting any house ready for sale is a huge undertaking. Agents who say you just need to clean up a bit may not be dedicated to the cause. On the flip side, agents that implore you to do major renovations may be going overboard.

And the Winner Is . . .

Now that you've interviewed a few agents, it's time to make a decision. Ask yourself the following questions:

1. Is this person accessible? There's nothing more frustrating than having an agent go AWOL on you. Make sure he or she returns calls (and e-mails if that's preferable to you). Better yet, have you been able to reach this agent directly by cell phone?

2. Do you want this person representing you? Were you comfortable with his appearance, style, temperament, and values? Does he seem well respected by other agents? Do you think he'll be a good negotiator?

3. Can you trust this person? Will you be comfortable sharing personal information with him? Are you confident that he'll protect your interests and be honest with you?

If you can answer yes to all of these questions, then you may have found your SOLDmate. But there's one more thing to do. Now it's time to determine the appropriate listing price for your home. This is obviously an important task along the road to SOLD, and the way that agents work with their clients to set listing prices says a lot about how they approach the entire process (and also gives a hint about how successful an agent they're likely to be).

SETTING THE LISTING PRICE

Quick question: What's your house worth? We assume a number just popped into your head. Now, ask yourself how you came up with that number. Maybe you looked on Zillow.com, or maybe a comparable house just sold for about that same amount. Or maybe you're just an eternal optimist and you absolutely love your house, so you think it's worth even more. The fact is, your answer might be a decent *approximation* of what your house is worth, but its true value can only be determined by one thing: exactly what the new owner will eventually pay for it. In our experience, setting the listing price as close to that amount as possible is the best strategy. Of course, you can't just call that person and ask them what they'll pay, so you've got to make an educated guess.

If you've done your homework and found the best agent for you, setting the listing price should be easy (and maybe even fun). What we normally do is ask our clients to write down what they think the listing price should be, and we do the same. Then, on the count of three, we reveal our prices. Usually we're pretty close, since we've educated our clients already about setting the price based on recent sales of comparable homes.

As a seller, you must resist the temptation to list your home higher than its approximate value. You may absolutely love your house and truly believe that it's worth more than the comparable sales your agent brings you, but that's not the way the market works. We'll see in Step 4 that some renovations may be personally valuable to you—you may have done the work yourself or the decorative objects have a personal significance—but that doesn't mean they're valuable to anyone else. One of the main reasons we tell sellers that they have to distance themselves emotionally from their homes is so they can price it properly (the other reason, as we'll see in Step 3, is so potential buyers can move in mentally).

This is a complicated concept, and something that sellers

Carrying Costs

We talk a lot in this book about the importance of time in relation to a successful sale. This is not just because a long, drawn-out listing can mess with your schedule and drive you nuts, but also because it costs you real money. Most sellers just focus on how much they made on the sale and don't notice how much they lost because it took longer to sell their house than it should have. Those "carrying costs" that they have to pay can include utilities, general maintenance fees, insurance, taxes, and most significantly, mortgage interest.

Every day that goes by with your house on the market is another day's interest collected by the bank on your loan. If you've owned your house for only a short time, that really adds up. For example, if you have a $350,000 loan at 6 percent for thirty years, and you've owned your house for two years, every month you pay about $1,700 in interest. So, if your house took three months to sell, instead of one, that's almost $3,500 extra in interest that you'll pay to the bank!

BUZZWORD

often disagree with us about, but we can't stress enough how important it is to follow our advice. (That's why we're repeating it!) If you list your house too far above the reasonably expected sale price, not only do you risk its taking longer to sell (which costs you real money as you continue to pay your current mortgage and other "carrying costs" longer; see "Buzzword: Carrying Costs"), but this may actually result in a *lower* sale price than if you had priced it correctly from the start.

Here's the scenario: Your house wallows on the market for months (you may get lots of showings initially, but that's probably because buyers' agents like showing overpriced houses so that properly priced ones will look good by comparison), and even if some fool comes along and offers your exorbitant price, you've got to deal with the appraisal. The buyer may be a fool, but we can guarantee that the bank won't be. It's unlikely that the bank will loan the buyer more money than the property's worth. Unless that buyer has a load of cash on hand, they won't get a big enough loan to close the deal. And at this point even a fool will realize that it's silly to pay more for a house than it's worth. The result for the seller is a dead deal.

Now you've got to relist the house, but it's got the added burden of the previous deal hanging over it. The stigma of that fiasco means your house is less attractive to buyers than it once was, and you're facing the prospect of selling for even less than the comps. If we've seen one constant in all of our experience in this business, it's that every time we tell a client that a house has been relisted, they immediately ask, "What's wrong with it?"

We've seen this so many times with clients who refuse to heed our warnings that now we won't work with clients who demand that we list too high. It's just too painful to see how devastated they are when they finally do close the sale and realize how much money they've lost.

We had clients who insisted on putting their house on the market at an inflated price "just to see what would happen." We warned them that what they would see is that nothing would happen. The house sat on the market for months with no activity, becoming "shelf stale." When a buyer finally did come in, the sellers were desperate to hold on to them and gave in on several key negotiating points. In the end, they left a ton of money on the table and the buyers ended up with a great deal.

Here's one final point to consider when setting the list price: most buyers have a very clear price range that they're considering, and their agent is not likely to show them listings outside that range. There aren't a lot of hard-and-fast rules in real estate, but one would definitely be that you'll never get an offer from someone who doesn't know your house is for sale. If you price your home too high, the buyers you're most hoping to attract may never even know it's for sale.

So stick to comparable sales when setting your price. If you've done valuable renovations and properly staged your house for sale (see Steps 4 and 5), the market will likely find a way to reward you with a quicker sale and more money. But before you take it to the market, it's time to sign the listing agreement and make it official with your SOLDmate.

THE LISTING AGREEMENT

Regardless of how comfortable you are with your agent, and how confident you are in his or her abilities, you must get everything in writing. The three major elements of the listing agreement follow.

Duration of the Agreement   Once again, this should be a few weeks longer than the average DOM for your area.

Commission   Standard commissions are 5–6 percent. Some discount brokerages may offer half that, so just be sure you know exactly what services they are and are not providing to you. Keep in mind that commissions are negotiable, but you want to be careful. Because of the current selling structure, where the listing agent splits the commission with the buyer's agent, there's a downside to negotiating a lower commission with your agent. In that case, buyers' agents are less likely to bring clients to your house over comparable houses with higher commissions. In a hot real estate market, that probably won't matter much, but in slower times it can hinder your sale.

List Price   Make sure you are completely comfortable with the price you and your agent agree upon before signing the agreement.

There are two other options you should request that your agent add to the agreement, assuming that they are not already included: an opt-out clause and a double-pop provision.

Opt-Out Clause   You should have the ability to end your relationship with this agent at any time if you are dissatisfied with her service. Keep in mind that some agents may include an exclusivity clause in the agreement, forbidding you from listing the house with another agent for a certain period of time after you terminate the agreement. We don't believe in this and strongly suggest sellers have such provisions removed before signing.

"Double-Pop" Provision   This refers to the instance when your agent also represents the buyer in the sale. As we mentioned previously, this transaction is too big and complex to have your agent representing both sides. We recommend that you include a clause in your agreement stating that your agent will cede representation of the buyer to another agent.

There are also a few pages of fine print and legalese in the listing agreement. One important clause gives agents a certain number of days after the listing expires to collect their commission if a buyer comes through who originally saw the house while it was listed with them. The standard for this is usually three to six months. Sellers should negotiate as short a time period as possible on this portion of the listing agreement. If you are uncomfortable with this or any other element of the listing agreement, do not hesitate to have your lawyer go over it and answer any questions you have.

WORKING TOGETHER

Your newly hired agent works for *you*. That means you've got a valuable asset in your corner, with all the benefits we talked about earlier. One possible downside to this relationship is that many real estate agents are hesitant to be brutally honest with their clients for fear of losing the listing. Suppose your boss asked for your opinion of the hideous tie his wife just gave him. Would you really tell him what you thought? You might, but only if you had an open and honest relationship with him. Even though you've found your SOLDmate, someone who really understands how to orchestrate a successful sale, it's still important to remember that as a seller, you're ultimately the boss, and it's up to you to set the tone of the relationship with your agent.

Start an Open Dialogue

It is vitally important for agents to speak their minds and put their experience into action. The best thing you can do as a seller is demand that your agent be frank with you, regardless of whether they think it might hurt your feelings. Remember, you're on the same team with the same goals. And everyone wants the best possible deal for your house.

To help get your relationship off to the right start, we've created the "Home Seller's Oath," opposite, that you can sign and give to your agent. This is a fun way to let them know you're serious about selling your house and that the two of you can work together to achieve the most successful sale.

Now that you've found your SOLDmate let's take a little time and get to know the folks who will be buying your home. Appreciating the buyers' motivations, concerns, and desires will help us focus on exactly what to do (and what not to do) to guarantee a successful sale.

The Home Seller's Oath

I, _____ , do hereby solemnly swear that I will approach the sale of my house objectively and will heed all advice given by my real estate agent, _____ .

I understand that, as a Seller, my house is no longer my home but a commodity to be sold unemotionally.

I am willing to forgo my personal style and taste, no matter how fantastic it is, in favor of staging my house to appeal to the greatest possible number of potential buyers.

I expect my agent to be brutally honest with me, knowing that we have a common goal: to get the best price from the best buyer as quickly as possible.

Therefore, I will not throw a tantrum, hold my breath and stomp my feet, or TP my agent's house if s/he does any of the following:

• Suggests that my paint colors look like something out of Willy Wonka's chocolate factory

• Forces me to pack away my priceless collection of Richard Nixon memorabilia or any other objects displayed in my house that may disturb potential buyers or prompt them to alert the local authorities

• Tells me that "keeping it natural" does not actually qualify as landscaping

• Disagrees with me when I suggest that buyers will like that "lived-in look" and tells me to "clean like I've never cleaned before!"

• Suggests anything else that her experience dictates I should do to improve my house for sale.

_____

Dedicated Seller(s)

3

Get Inside the Buyer's Mind

THE PREVIOUS CHAPTERS have really been about taking your role as a seller seriously and committing yourself fully to the process. You have gotten to know yourself as a seller and have presumably developed an appreciation for the complexity of selling a home. This chapter looks at the whole process from the other side.

Any good businessperson will tell you how essential it is to know your customers. What are their motivations, their fears, and their goals? Since you're now in the business of selling a home (we hope we can help make it a very short, prosperous career), it's important to take some time to get to know *your* customer: the prospective home buyer. Understanding the buyer will influence everything you do from this point forward and will hopefully result in a financially and personally rewarding sale.

Let's face it, you can do everything right and be selling in the greatest seller's market ever known, but it all amounts to nothing unless you get the buyer's signature at closing. You cannot ever take buyers for granted, and you must respect the power that they ultimately have. To do so, you should put yourself in their shoes.

REMEMBER WHEN YOU WERE BUYING?

Many sellers quickly forget what life as a buyer was like. Buyers feel so much anxiety and excitement, but it all is quickly forgotten once they settle into their new home. It's worthwhile to think about just what the buyers are going through, so let's see if we can take you back to those long-ago days. Picture yourself sitting down for breakfast on a sunny Sunday morning, the table strewn with newspaper.

- You're fed up with looking through the Sunday Real Estate section.

- You don't think you'll ever find the perfect home.

- You've had at least a few fights with your significant other over this.

- You see the same frustrated faces at the open houses week after week.

- You've fallen in love with a few places, only to be outbid.

- Every month it gets more painful to write that rent check.

- The market seems to be getting hotter and hotter, pricing you out of more and more homes. Or, the market is cooling and you're not sure you should buy.

- You start thinking about all the things you'll have to give up in order to scrape a down payment together.

- You've seen so many houses that you can't distinguish one from the other anymore.

- You have no idea if you can actually afford any of this.

- Maybe you've been forced to relocate and suddenly you have to find a new place to call home, and fast!

In other words, being a prospective buyer is a pretty tumultuous experience. Most buyers are insecure, frustrated, and probably a good bit scared. Worst of all, they're as exposed personally and financially as they've probably ever been.

THE NAKED BUYER

We often say that the process of buying a house is like standing naked in front of a mirror. Or, more accurately, it's like standing naked in front of everyone you know, and a few people you've just recently met.

Even the Pros Get Nervous

Shannon recently went through the process of buying a home. You would think her experience in the business would relieve her of all the typical buyer's fears. You'd be wrong . . .

Donna: When Shannon bought her house, she was a lunatic!

Shannon: Hey! I was not a lunatic. Maybe a maniac, but that's not quite the same thing.

Donna: I remember she'd found an article in the paper saying that the market was softening, and she called me in the middle of the night. "Mom, did I just make a huge mistake?" she asked. I was able to talk her down from the ledge.

Shannon: It was amazing, even after helping so many people buy their own homes, I was still so uncertain when I was the buyer. I knew the market inside and out, better than any of my clients ever could, and I still wasn't sure I'd made the right decision.

Donna: Imagine how uncertain nonprofessionals will be. It's a good thing we buy and sell *other people's* homes for a living and not our own; otherwise, we'd be total basket cases.

BUYER'S EYES

Finances

The most obvious exposure that buyers feel is financial. Suddenly they know exactly how much money they have—and how much they don't have. They also come face to face with their personal debt and their credit rating. People who previously spent their days blissfully unaware of their financial status suddenly know every detail, and it's the rare individual who is completely happy with what they see.

Buyers also realize that the details of their finances are unexpectedly very public. They've probably applied for mortgage pre-approval, and along the way any number of people have seen their bank statements, pay stubs, and investment information. Many buyers find it particularly disconcerting to know that their real estate agent learns so much about their finances.

Finally, there's a tremendous amount of financial uncertainty involved in a home purchase. Especially for first time buyers, it's almost impossible to know exactly what your monthly outlay will be, plus nobody can accurately predict the market. If you stop to think about it, and most buyers do, it's really a huge leap of faith.

Personal Lives

In addition to the financial exposure, there are also innumerable personal details that surface. We've seen couples discover just how different they really are while buying a house. They might have different tastes, different risk tolerances, and different priorities. Moreover, extended family often gets involved, which is always an adventure. Parents can agree to provide the down payment, and then they find that they don't like the house and opt not to help out financially.

We had one client pull us aside during the loan application process and practically beg us not to tell her husband about a prior bankruptcy she'd never told him about. We felt really bad for her, but there was nothing that we could do to keep that information from coming out. Every time we help another client buy a house we're amazed to see just how personally revealing this process is.

Leaping into the Great Unknown

Beyond feeling exposed financially and personally, buyers are faced with a huge information deficit: namely, just how much this whole transaction is going to cost them. Every day, it seems, buyers find out about a new fee or service charge that somebody wants, and they don't know if or when those charges will ever stop. At best, they can get a general sense of their mortgage payments, but rates fluctuate and it's virtually impossible to get an exact figure. Then there's insurance, property taxes, and utilities to consider, which are also virtually impossible to know exactly. And the mortgage interest deduction offers precious little comfort, since the payback is a long way off and most buyers get headaches just thinking about it.

We had a recent client who contacted us the morning of the home inspection and told us he wanted to back out of the deal. He hadn't slept in days and showed us page after page of scribbled calculations, as he tried to figure out what all this would cost. Eventually, he just couldn't take the uncertainty of it all and decided it was too big a risk. Luckily, we were able to calm him down, and after going through the numbers with him, we were able to show him that it wasn't that great a risk after all. We still get e-mails from him thanking us for helping him with the best financial decision he's ever made. Today, he's a savvy real estate investor, but back then he was a nervous wreck.

Gone Bananas, and Then He Split

Here's an example of just how stressful the buying process can become. We represented a couple buying a multimillion-dollar property, and yet the husband kept asking us about two of the windows. They needed to be replaced, but it certainly wasn't a big issue given the scale of the transaction. And yet he was so concerned about the windows and how much they might cost to replace that he and his wife agreed that they just couldn't go through with the purchase. It was that one added uncertainty, on top of everything else, that changed their minds. It turned out later that he was just using the windows as an issue to keep from buying the house because he wanted to split up with his wife. But the fact that she agreed with him and scuttled the sale just shows how powerful the uncertainty within the buying process can be. Of course, we don't advocate using that uncertainty for devious personal agendas, but as you can see it is possible to do so.

WHAT DOES ALL THIS MEAN FOR SELLERS?

As you can see, buyers find themselves completely exposed, uninformed, naked before the world, about to embark on the biggest financial commitment of their lives (a commitment that for many of them will last longer than any other relationship).

To say the least, they're not entering into this casually. Even the most risk-tolerant gambler wants to make sure everything feels right before signing those loan papers. Prospective buyers look for reassurance, and many times they'll fixate on any uncertainty and imperfection. If they see a dripping faucet, they'll assume all the

There's so much on the buyer's mind that even the smallest thing can send him over the edge.

BUYER'S EYES

Domestic Disasters

There's a wonderful story by Spalding Gray called "Terrors of Pleasure," about his efforts to buy the "perfect $30,000 cabin" in the Catskills. When he begins looking at houses, the sellers are always home, and he finds himself becoming more and more interested in the little domestic scenes he's interrupting rather than seriously thinking about buying the property. When you're selling, you don't want buyers to think about you and your life in the house. In Gray's case it was entertaining, but for most buyers it's intimidating.

For example, we just spoke with a buyer who recently went to an open house and the seller's *entire family* was there watching television. She felt like an intruder in the house and wanted nothing more than just to get out of there as quickly as possible.

FOOL'S FABLE

plumbing is bad. If there's a patch on the roof, they assume it means the whole roof could cave in at any minute. Sellers must not allow the seeds of doubt to take root in prospective buyers. It's too easy for that negative energy to snowball until they want out.

As we'll see later on, there are countless things you can do to prepare your house for the market. Many of those tasks are intended to specifically improve the buyer's state of mind. Let's take a look at five of those tasks that we'll discuss later in greater detail, and see exactly how they can help put the buyers at ease.

TOP FIVE WAYS TO PUT BUYERS AT EASE

1. Leave the house. Most buyers feel like they're intruding if the sellers are home. You want them to "move in mentally" right away and not feel self-conscious about moving through the house with you peering over their shoulder.

2. Get a lockbox. Having a lockbox makes it very easy for buyers' agents to get into the house for showings. It just eliminates one more potential unknown for buyers, and we can't stress enough the psychological impact of making the process as easy as possible for them.

3. Turn on the lights. This might seem like a minor point, but it's crucial to the showing experience. You want buyers to immediately feel at ease and at home as soon as they walk through the door. Then they can start looking around and exploring on their own. Otherwise, they enter into a dark room, while their agent fumbles around for the light switch. They end up following their agent around throughout the house, never quite feeling comfortable. Also, you can have music playing and light candles ahead of time (just make sure they're safe and secure and won't light the drapes on fire).

4. Contain the pets. This is similar to turning on the lights. You don't want a buyer's agent to be wrestling with your dog while their clients look on aghast.

5. Clean, clean, clean. Basically, you want your home to look like it's ready for a dinner party. So, when buyers arrive they enter into a clean, warm, friendly, and well-lit home that they can settle into.

What They Don't Know Can Scare Them

Given the enormity and uncertainty of even an average real estate transaction, it's amazing that any properties ever actually sell. Buyers ultimately need to make a leap of faith and commit to something they'll never know everything about. Sometimes, of course, their fears get the best of them. In Southern California and in many other warm-weather locales, just about every property built with wood has some degree of a termite problem. It comes with the territory. We recently had a client from Portland, Oregon, where even the suspicion of termites is a deal breaker, who became obsessed with the little critters. He saw termites as the cause of every imperfection in the house—he even told us he had termite nightmares—and ultimately couldn't bring himself to buy any of the houses we showed him. This may sound extreme, but we see this kind of behavior all the time with buyers.

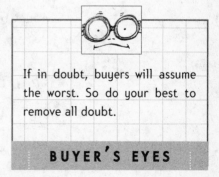

If in doubt, buyers will assume the worst. So do your best to remove all doubt.

BUYER'S EYES

We'll explain in Steps 4 and 5 just how to get your house ready for even the most fidgety buyer. For now, though, let's get to know the types of buyers who are out there, and get a better sense of just what they're looking for.

TYPES OF BUYERS: THE GOOD, THE BAD, AND THE DOWNRIGHT UGLY

We've come up with nine general categories of prospective buyers. There certainly could be individuals who fit into more than one category, and some buyers out there occupy new and unique categories all by themselves. But these groups capture the vast majority of buyers and will help us figure out exactly what we need to do to attract the greatest possible number of them.

First-Time Buyers

Code Name   Rookies

Profile   Rookies are usually rather cautious. Any abnormalities will get their attention. Because they've never owned a home before, they probably don't know how to distinguish a minor cosmetic issue from a structural problem. They're usually strapped for cash, and a thirty-year mortgage feels like a lifetime commitment. Also, there's a good chance they're getting all or part of their down payment from relatives, which can really make things interesting. Money from relatives almost always comes with a lot of unsolicited advice, which can easily overwhelm an already stressed-out buyer.

What They Want   They want value, a solid property without any extravagances or uncertainties.

Single Professionals

Code Name   The Suits

Profile   These are young go-getters who may travel a lot, make a lot of money, and are possibly looking for a tax write-off.

What They Want   They don't need a lot of space and certainly don't need big kitchens. If there's an extra bedroom they'll likely convert it into an office. They want to be able to just shut the door behind them and head out of town without worrying about anything. On the other hand, some Suits may be looking for "status" homes, likely in the McMansion mold.

Buyers Who Have Outgrown Their House
Code Name   Brady Bunchers

Profile   These are buyers for whom family concerns are paramount. They're likely to be experienced buyers, with a bit more financial security than Rookies.

What They Want   They're probably looking for a long-term house, something that meets the needs of their growing family and will get them through the high school years. Space is essential, although they also might be interested in expanding in a few years. They're less interested in fancy details than solid, child-resistant construction. Storage is also important, as well as a yard. Location, particularly regarding local schools, is a top priority.

Relocators
Code Name   Journeymen

Profile   Journeymen are primarily people who are moving long distances because of work, although they can also move for family or retirement reasons. The key factors influencing them are time and unfamiliarity with the new market. Particularly for job-related relocations, timing is key. These folks are usually on a tight schedule and have to sell their current house before buying a new one. For just about all relocators, there's little knowledge of the new market. They're unfamiliar with the neighborhoods and often have to overcome significant sticker shock (although sometimes they're pleasantly surprised if they're moving to a cheaper market). Also, they can be looking to buy at any time of the year, since relocations are usually not seasonally dependent.

What They Want   Most Journeymen are looking for houses in move-in condition. Their time constraints and lack of knowledge tend to keep them away from fixer-uppers. People moving for family or retirement may have their own particular interests, depending on their personal situations, but they also tend to want houses in near-perfect condition.

Lifestyle-Change Buyers
Code Name   Downsizers

Profile   This category includes parents whose children have just moved away ("empty-nest" buyers) and buyers coming out of a divorce or the death of a spouse. For the most part these buyers tend to be more mature and require less space.

What They Want   These folks are obviously looking for less square footage and probably one-level homes for older buyers. They're not interested in fixer-uppers. They want lots of storage for all the stuff they've accumulated over the years, plus a spare room or rooms so the kids (and grandkids) can come and visit.

"Why Remodel, Just Replace" Buyers
Code Name   Mr. and Mrs. Clean

All Buyers Are Welcome

The key when preparing your house is not to exclude *any* potential buyers and to keep in mind that your house is likely to appeal to at least two or more of the nine types of buyers. For example, we had clients recently who were expecting their second child and decided to sell and find a larger place. When their first daughter was born, they decorated her nursery like something out of *Sesame Street*. When they went to sell, it was essential that they not exclude potential buyers without children, so we helped them tone down their daughter's room to make it obvious that the room could also serve as a guest room or an office (see Step 5 for specific strategies to stage your house so it appeals to the broadest possible range of buyers).

Profile   These are folks who have contemplated expanding or renovating their current homes and decided they'd rather just buy a new place and save themselves the hassle of pulling permits, dealing with contractors, and so on. They tend to have lots of equity in the current home. Some Brady Bunchers may also fall into this category.

What They Want   These folks are in the market for a "bring your toothbrush" house (that is, all you need to do is bring your toothbrush and you can move right in). In some cases they want to buy more square footage rather than expand their current house, or they just want a brand-new version of their current place. You know the way new construction has a gleam about it, from the perfect plaster to the shiny appliances (sort of like the "new car smell" of real estate)? Well, that's what these folks want.

Rental Property Buyers
Code Name   The Ropers

Profile   These buyers are real estate investors, although they may include buyers looking for vacation homes that they'll rent out for most of the year. They approach the sale impersonally and are only thinking of the bottom line.

What They Want   These buyers may or may not want a place that needs work, but ultimately they want a property that will be sufficient for tenants. They're looking for clean, basic homes that will be easy to maintain. The phrase they might use is "something that makes sense."

Buyer Who Want to Fix Up and Sell Fast
Code Name   Flippers

Profile   These are the day traders of real estate, the serious players looking to make a quick profit.

What They Want   Flippers are usually looking for places that need cosmetic work, so they can quickly dress the place up for resale, although some may be interested in more extensive renovations. They want to close quickly, so they can get in and start prepping the house for resale.

Vacation Home Buyers
Code Name   Weekenders

Profile   These folks tend to be older and more financially secure. They're definitely experienced buyers.

What They Want Obviously, location is most important to these people. They're looking for a perfect getaway near the beach, in the mountains, or wherever they want to escape to. For sellers, it will be pretty obvious if your home would be of interest to these buyers. If yours qualifies, remember that they may be interested in buying the place fully furnished.

NOW that we've explored the full range of buyers based on what they're looking for, it's time to learn what kind of business partners they'll be (remember, for the time being you're in the home-selling business). Specifically, you need to know the warning signs when you're dealing with a potentially troublesome buyer.

IF YOU MEET THESE BUYERS, BEWARE!

The vast majority of prospective buyers are rational, considerate people. But every once in a while you'll encounter a buyer who seems intent on making your life miserable—someone you just know will be trouble. It's important to recognize these buyers quickly, and be prepared to deal with them. Let's take a look at the most common types of problem buyers and what you'll need to do to protect yourself, your investment, and your sanity.

Buyers Who Have Been Looking Full Time for over Six Months

What's the Deal? All buyers eventually learn that there's no such thing as a perfect house. Those who take more than six months to figure this out are not really serious about buying.

What to Do You and your agent have to keep a really short leash on these buyers. They're likely to back out of the deal at any time. They'll probably want a lot of contingencies included in their offer, so make sure your real estate agent is a strong negotiator and keeps everything moving along smoothly.

Contingencies

Contingencies are requirements that either the buyer or seller places in the contract, which must be met within a certain period of time in order for the transaction to proceed. For example, most buyers require that their offer is contingent upon the completion of a home inspection, and afterward both parties will negotiate how to respond to the inspector's findings. Other common contingencies include an appraisal contingency, which protects the buyer if the home appraises for less than the agreed-upon sale price, and a contingency that protects buyers who need to sell their current house before buying a new one. For more information on the practical impact of contingencies, see Step 6.

BUZZWORD

Bottom Feeders

What's the Deal?   We define a bottom feeder as any buyer who submits an offer 20 percent or more below the listing price (assuming that the property was originally priced correctly). There are two main types of bottom feeders out there.

First, there is the serial bottom feeder, who just goes around submitting extremely low offers with the hope of finding a bargain. They don't seriously think the house is only worth as much as they're offering but that they may get lucky.

Second, there is the accidental bottom feeder. This is a buyer who is just inexperienced and has a gut feeling that the property is worth much less than the listing price. The buyer's agent may disagree but is obligated nonetheless to submit the offer. These types of bottom feeders tend to learn very quickly that their gut feelings aren't always accurate.

What to Do   First of all, do not get offended and do not assume an extremely low offer means you overpriced your house. This type of offer is just a part of doing business, and if you've followed our advice your home should be appropriately priced.

We recommend that your agent tell the buyer that their offer is too low (do not come down from your listing price). Simply invite the buyer to submit a new, higher offer. For more information on negotiations and accepting an offer, see Step 6.

Buyers Who Have Not Been Prequalified

What's the Deal?   While it's possible that these buyers are perfectly qualified and have just decided to make an offer without being *pre*qualified, smart and serious buyers know that savvy sellers will demand a prequalification letter before taking their home off the market.

What to Do   Your risk here is that their financing will fall through, so you've got to be vigilant. Make sure your agent insists that the buyers' loan contingencies are as short as possible, and make sure their offer includes evidence of their ability to make a down payment. Make sure they've proven to you that they're actually able to buy your house before you accept their offer.

Prequalification Letter

A prequalification letter is written from a lending institution stating that based on a review of the appropriate information, the buyer is qualified to borrow enough money to purchase a particular piece of property. It is proof of the financial potential of the buyer.

BUZZWORD

Proof of Down Payment

Proof of down payment is similar to a prequalification letter, but rather than showing your financial potential, it shows what you've already got. Specifically, it shows that you have sufficient funds at hand to make the down payment on the property. Proof of down payment usually takes the form of a bank or investment account statement.

BUZZWORD

Buyers Who Won't Show Proof of Down Payment

What's the Deal?   If buyers are hesitant to show you proof of their down payment, it usually means they don't have it. We can't think of any other reason why a serious, qualified buyer would withhold this important information.

What to Do   We suggest that sellers require proof of down payment, as well as a prequalifying letter from a reputable bank before accepting an offer. A good agent will make this a contingency with a very short time frame.

Buyers Who Don't Follow Through

What's the Deal?   If buyers miss appointments or their agents don't return phone calls promptly, it usually means the buyer and/or their agent is a flake or they're not seriously interested in closing the sale. We have a zero-tolerance policy for flakes. That doesn't mean we won't work with these people or accept their offers, but it means we take an absolute no-more-nonsense approach with them.

What to Do   Be sure your agent sticks to the letter of the law with these folks, and if they don't comply, then bail out. As soon as they realize you're not playing games, they will likely become much more responsive or decide to cancel the sale, which will make your home available for a serious buyer.

Buyers Who Represent Themselves

What's the Deal?   We've seen this a handful of times over the years, and it never ceases to make our heads spin. In areas where buyers don't pay any commission to their agents they've really got nothing to lose and everything to gain by working with an agent.

What to Do   This situation screams "Lawsuit!" to us. There's just so much that could go wrong. These folks tend to be compulsive negotiators who always have something to prove, regardless of how it affects the transaction. A few years back we had clients who accepted an offer from a buyer who was representing himself. He put a $20,000 good-faith deposit into escrow and we wrote a seventeen-day loan contingency into the offer. He was a busy guy, and not terribly organized, and he wasn't able to get the loan together. Because the sellers had taken their home off the market and the buyer was unable to perform, the sellers had the right to keep his deposit. This buyer demanded his deposit back and threatened to sue for the money. It got ugly and the buyer lost a considerable amount of money. This would have been totally avoidable if he had had an agent working exclusively for him and watching the calendar and his time frames. Luckily, we had another buyer lined up. We ended up selling the home to another buyer with a very smooth transaction.

In most cases, we suggest not accepting any independent offers, although in a few very rare instances it may be worth pursuing. If a buyer comes to the table ready to pay cash, and she wants to close within a couple of days, you can probably entertain her offer. Even still, you should work very closely with your agent and keep a short leash on the buyer if this situation arises.

Buyers Who Need to Sell Before They Can Buy

What's the Deal?　Many buyers need to sell the house they're in before they can get the down payment together on a new home. If the timing is particularly tight, they'll require that you wait to schedule closing until their current home closes as well. This invariably makes the entire process much more stressful.

What to Do　These buyers may be perfectly honest and upstanding, and the sale of their current home may be a sure thing, but this contingency adds a new layer of uncertainty into an already uncertain process. The quality of their offer may outweigh the added stress, but in many cases it won't. Of course, in a buyer's market you might have to accept that uncertainty, but in a seller's market we recommend that our sellers stay away. Talk it over with your agent and make sure you're completely comfortable before accepting this contingency. Keep in mind that many buyers will need to sell their current homes and you don't want to alienate them, but also remember that the time you spend waiting to close costs you real money.

THE BUYERS' CYCLE

The last aspect of buyers' motivations that we'll explore is timing. You can learn a lot about buyers, and therefore maximize your chances of successful selling, by understanding the best seasons in which to sell. Let's take a stroll through a typical calendar year and see what's on buyers' minds as the seasons go by.

January

What's Up?   While there may not be huge numbers of prospective buyers looking around in the dead of winter, those who are have probably been putting off any serious consideration since October owing to the craziness of the holiday season. So after the first of the year we do see an increase in activity.

Who's Looking?   The Suits have just gotten their year-end bonuses and could be ready to buy. Most Brady Bunchers traditionally wait until summer to buy, so the kids won't have their school years disrupted. But some may find that moving in the spring allows their kids to meet new friends so they don't spend the summer alone. Also, Weekenders may start looking for summer places at this time.

February & March

What's Up?   This is tax time. People meet with their accountants and realize they need some tax relief, and if interest rates are good, their mortgage interest deduction may allow them to own for the same cost as renting. Also, tax refunds can help people get their down payments together. Current owners may figure out that they can cash out of their existing homes, realize significant tax benefits, and purchase a new home. This is a really good time to put your house on the market, since demand is picking up rapidly, and you can catch these prospective buyers at the peak of their interest.

Who's Looking?　This is a good season for Weekenders, Flippers, and the Ropers. Also, Mr. and Mrs. Clean may have finally convinced themselves that their finances are right to buy the perfect, new place. Basically, anyone for whom financial benefits are paramount is likely to become an active buyer at this time of year.

April to August

What's Up?　This is high season for just about everyone. Everyone's got a little more time to devote to looking for a home. With school out of session, most families with children are looking to move before the new school year starts.

Who's Looking?　Everyone.

September to December

What's Up?　With school starting up again, and the relaxed pace of summer just a memory, the time and interest in real estate slows dramatically. Once the holidays appear on the horizon, the market can go stone cold.

Who's Looking?　While no groups are predictably active this season, there are always people who have to move. Sudden job changes or unforeseen personal changes are the main culprits. Therefore, you're most likely to find Suits and Downsizers looking at this time. Most important for sellers to realize, if you do put your house on the market at this time, while you will get fewer interested buyers, those you do find will be serious, motivated buyers.

NOW that you know the who, why, and when of prospective buyers, you'll have a good sense of the likely customers for your house. Now we can dig into the details of what you'll need to do to get these perfect buyers to sign on the dotted line.

LET THEM MOVE IN MENTALLY

As we'll see in Step 5, you want to create the look of a model home when you prepare your house for the market. If you've never been to a model home, it's worth checking one out. The two most obvious characteristics of model homes are that they are perfect and impersonal. They're sort of like fashion models; the best ones are great to look at, but they don't exhibit any real character or expression. That way you can impart upon them any emotion you want, which makes them all the more alluring (to paraphrase author Milan Kundera). With a model home, the impersonal nature allows visitors to easily visualize themselves living there.

So, when you're preparing your own house, you want to move yourself out as much as possible. That doesn't mean clearing out the furniture and the dishes, but you should make your home as impersonal as possible. Otherwise, prospective buyers will feel as if they are intruding in your home rather than creating a mental image of their own.

Picking the Right Words

One way to utilize your understanding of the buyer's mind-set is to use the right words in your listing and avoid the bad ones. This is something that any good agent should have mastered, but since nobody knows your house better than you do, you should be able to contribute as well. But which are the right words?

Here's a little quiz for you. Which of the following words should you include in your listing description, and which should you avoid?

Gourmet	Granite
State-of-the-art	Charming
Great neighborhood	Fantastic
Corian	

An analysis of real estate ads by Steven Levitt and Stephen Dubner in *Freakonomics* found that more specific words that describe the house itself—granite, Corian, gourmet, and state-of-the-art—correlated with higher sale prices. The more ambiguous terms, or those that didn't describe the house itself—charming, great neighborhood, and fantastic—correlated with lower sale prices. From a buyer's perspective, the results are not at all surprising.

A 2005 *House & Garden* real estate survey found that 70 percent of those polled preferred a new house to a previously owned home. Therefore, specific features that give the impression of newness (even if the house is not new) will appeal to buyers. They give buyers a good sense of what the house is like even before they see it.

More important, ambiguous terms plant seeds of doubt in the buyer's mind. They get suspicious that you're hiding something, and they approach the house (if they visit it at all) much more cautiously and skeptically.

Whether you're the type of seller who wants to micromanage the entire process, or if you'd rather sit back and let your agent handle everything, it's worth looking over the listing description to make sure it's worded optimally.

Be specific when describing your home, and avoid ambiguous or empty words. If you mention a brand by name (e.g., Jacuzzi) make sure that you actually have that exact brand.

INSIDER SECRET

NOW that you have a thorough understanding of the people involved—yourself, your agent, and the buyers—it's time to shift your focus to the other player in our little drama: the actual house.

4

Remodel, Repair, and Renew

IN THE NEXT two chapters we'll focus on the house itself and show you how to best prepare it to go on the market. Step 4 deals primarily with significant improvements and fixes to your house; Step 5 will help you prepare your house to welcome prospective buyers and their agents.

REMODEL

We usually don't suggest that sellers focus on major renovations when they're getting ready to sell. As we'll see, it's unlikely you'll make a sizable return on the investment, and the hassle of tearing apart your house just as you're getting ready to sell and move out can be a major inconvenience. But there are instances when you should seriously consider renovating.

Keeping Up with the Joneses

Remodeling that brings your house up to the local standards can really pay off. For example, if most of the nearby homes have two and a half baths, but you only have one and a half, converting that half bath to a full and possibly even adding an extra half bath is worth serious consideration. Buyers and their agents definitely notice these types of disparities, and you don't want to find yourself on the wrong side of an unflattering comparison.

Living Well Is Reward Enough

If you're at least a couple of years away from selling, and you'll enjoy the benefits of the renovation while you're still living there, it can definitely be worthwhile. But in this case you shouldn't count on getting a great return on investment (ROI) for your renovations. Your reward is the comfort and luxury of living in a renovated home. While you're likely to get some return on your renovation investment, your ROI will obviously decrease as more time passes between the improvement and the sale.

The Drive to DIY

If you're the do-it-yourself (DIY) type and just love doing renovations (and you don't mind living without a kitchen or bathroom for a while), we won't stand in your way. To each his own, we always say. Doing things yourself (assuming you do them well) is a great way to dramatically lower the cost of renovations and pretty much ensure a decent return on your investment.

Keep in mind that there are also a few important factors that could negatively affect the ROI for home renovations, including the following.

A Renovation That Sticks Out   If your entire house needs work, you're better off spreading your renovation dollars throughout the home rather than focusing on one room. For example, you might spend tens of thousands of dollars updating a kitchen in a house that was built in the 1970s and really shows its age. But rather than the new kitchen drawing attention away from the rest of the house, it is more likely to cause prospective buyers to focus on the rest of the house, which now looks even more dilapidated by comparison with the kitchen.

Overrenovation   Just as you can have too much of a good thing, overrenovating can be a waste of money. There's a saying that when buyers start thinking about their own return on investment, they want to buy the cheapest house in the best neighborhood that they can afford. That's not to suggest that you want your house to be the cheapest on the block, just that many buyers are wary of paying top dollar to buy the best house on the block. That means making your house significantly "better" than others around it — adding bedrooms, bathrooms, or upscale features not common in nearby homes — is not only unlikely to earn you a good return on your investment, but it might even hinder your prospects by making your house seem overpriced by comparison with others in your area.

There Are Always Trade-Offs

We know some of you are sitting there thinking, "Are these gals crazier than they look? I don't have the time or the desire to do any minor repairs—let alone major renovations—before I put my house on the market. What pearls of wisdom do they have for someone like me?"

First of all, we totally understand that each seller's situation is unique, and that some people simply cannot follow most (or any) of our recommendations for preparing their houses. That's fine, but to preserve your sanity throughout this process, make sure your goals reflect this (see "Rank Your Goals Again" in Step 1). For example, sellers who, for whatever reason, need to put their houses on the market as-is cannot possibly expect to get the highest price. There are always trade-offs, and you have to be honest with yourself and realistic in your expectations.

Some sellers believe that listing their house as-is will somehow result in a smoother transaction, since buyers will understand going into it that the sellers will be making no repairs to the home. Unfortunately, that's usually just not the case. When buyers see an as-is listing, they start salivating like Pavlov's dog. They can smell a bargain and a motivated seller, and they'll usually approach the entire transaction more aggressively. On top of all that, listing your house in this way does not prevent the buyer from completing a home inspection and requesting that defects be fixed or credit for repairs be given after his offer is accepted, nor will it prevent him from exercising his right to cancel the sale based on a contingency clause of the sales agreement (see "Contingencies" in Step 6).

If you truly don't have the time or energy to fully prepare your house for the market, at the very least you should remove as much of the clutter as you possibly can, hire a cleaning crew for the interior, and a gardener or landscaper to clean up the outside. Also, make sure your agent knows how much (or how little) you are able to do, so he or she can leverage whatever resources are available to help you out.

MAKE YOUR PLACE MEMORABLE

When we work with buyers, we often find that they latch on to one or two features of a given house to help them distinguish it from all the others they've seen. Buyers are busy people in a crazy period in their lives. They've seen so many houses that they can't remember which was which. The more you can do to make your house stand out, the better off you're likely to be.

There's only so much you can change about the fundamental structure of the house. And as we've said, we don't really recommend undertaking major renovations just before selling. But there are some things you can do to make an impression on buyers without expending significant effort or cost. We've come up with a list of our favorite features that are really cool, useful, and reasonably cheap (at least relative to a kitchen or bathroom remodel). We don't recommend that you go out of your way to add these things, but if you're doing similar improvements they're worth considering. If you already have any of these or similar memorable items, make sure they're in excellent condition so that buyers take away nothing but fond memories.

Twelve Little Things That Can Make a Big Impression

1. Pot filler. A pot filler is simply a water spigot mounted on the wall behind the stove. It is used to fill pots placed on the stove, rather than having to fill them in the sink and then carry them to the stove full of water. This little feature is the ultimate add-on: it will probably only cost you a couple hundred dollars, it is actually quite useful, and everyone who sees it thinks it is just the coolest thing. We've seen people walk into state-of-the-art kitchens with all the stainless-steel appliances and All-Clad cookware, and they immediately fall in love with the pot filler.

We wouldn't suggest that you call the plumber today and start ripping out your kitchen walls, but if you're doing some plumbing work in there anyway, and there's easy access to a water line near the stove, it's an option well worth exploring.

2. Instant hot-water dispenser. This is a nice little feature that allows you to have near-boiling water at the press of a button. If you've got a soap dispenser installed next to your faucet and you haven't used it in years, you may want to take that out and replace it with a hot water dispenser. This little appliance allows buyers to imagine all the conveniences they'll have access to once they move in for real.

3. Wine fridge. This may seem like an unnecessary luxury, but that's exactly the point. A wine fridge can give your house a big dose of indulgence without a major investment. Some models can easily be installed under your kitchen countertop, but we wouldn't recommend removing any kitchen cabinets unless you've got plenty of other kitchen storage available.

4. Cabinet lights. In this case we're talking about lighting either inside or underneath your kitchen cabinets. Inside lighting can be a bit more expensive and complicated to install, but it does lend an air of elegance to an otherwise mundane space. Unfortunately, inside cabinet lights are pretty much useless unless you have glass cabinet doors. Additionally, installing lights means that the interiors of the cabinets are completely visible (and therefore need to be kept that much more neat and clean).

Under-cabinet lights can be installed quite easily and cheaply. And, since even the most well-lit kitchen is bound to have some shadow spots underneath the cabinets, lighting under there can be a very practical addition to the workspace.

5. Tubular skylights (or solar tubes). Skylights are a wonderful way to add natural light to your home, but in many locations they're impractical or impossible to install. Tubular skylights can be installed just about anywhere for a reasonable price. This type of skylight includes a fixture on the roof to capture the sunlight, a flexible channel to direct the light into the house, and an outlet fixture in the ceiling, which looks much like a normal light fixture. For more information, visit www.solatube.com.

6. Cedar closet. Cedar paneling can be a beautiful and practical addition to any closet. It has a dark, rich color with a pronounced grain, and its oil is repellent to moths and other insects, protecting your clothing and linen. You have a variety of options for adding the benefits of cedar to a closet, from small planks hung with your clothes to panel-ing on the entire closet interior. The only maintenance that cedar re-quires is a light sanding whenever the scent fades, usually no more frequently than once or twice a year. Another nice advantage of cedar paneling is that it's relatively simple to install. You can pick up the paneling at a Lowe's or Home Depot, and they should be able to ex-plain how to install it.

A cedar closet doesn't just look good; it can also indicate to pros-pective buyers that you're a responsible homeowner who cares about your possessions. That's a belief you definitely want to encourage as buyers consider bidding on your house.

7. Closet lights. If you plan on having any electrical work done as you prepare to sell your house, closet lights are an inexpensive im-provement that can make a big difference (especially after you pick up all the dirty clothes strewn all over the closet floor). We're not sug-gesting you add lights to every closet, but if you have a closet that is easily accessible and used often, they're worth considering. Basically, if there's enough room for a light fixture—go ahead and add it. Closet lights will make the space feel larger and also offer a small, pleasant surprise to prospective buyers when they light up the space and get a good look at it (thus, the necessity of diligently cleaning it beforehand).

8. Spare fridge (and maybe even an extra dishwasher). If you're thinking about replacing your kitchen appliances, it might be worth keeping your old fridge and putting it in the garage or in the base-ment. Regardless of how organized you are, it's easy to fill up a fridge (especially if you have kids). It's just an added convenience that can appeal to buyers. The lifestyle that the extra refrigerator represents helps buyers move in mentally.

If you want to go really upscale, and you have the space in your kitchen, a second dishwasher can seem like the ultimate in domestic indulgence. The extra appliance would be most useful when entertaining, so you can run one dishwasher and keep the other available for the dirty dishes. This is a great, if somewhat impractical way to help buyers imagine how great it would be to live in your home.

9. Fruit trees. Even out here in California where our neighbors have everything from lemons and limes to avocados and figs, it's still really cool whenever we see a fruit tree in someone's yard. Buyers immediately think about the pies they'll bake or the fruit they'll pick and eat right off the tree. The main issue with fruit trees is that they tend to be less attractive than ornamental trees. So you probably don't want to plant an entire orchard in your backyard, just a select few trees.

10. Epoxy-coated garage floor. We don't usually recommend spending too much time and money fixing up garages, since most buyers these days want to know that there is a garage, but they're not overly concerned about the quality of it. But these floor coatings can take an otherwise overlooked space and easily make it memorable. An important side effect of resurfacing your garage floor is that it requires you to completely empty your garage. This in turn will probably free up a lot of storage space, which will help you declutter the rest of the house.

11. Outdoor/kitchen speakers. We have a client who recently did a complete kitchen renovation, with stainless steel appliances, beautiful natural-wood cabinets with frosted glass panes, and spotless hardwood floors. Even with all of that, his favorite features are far and away the speakers he installed in the kitchen ceiling. He has music playing in his house all the time, and it's a wonderful effect to have it follow you from the living room into the kitchen.

This can be a complicated procedure, depending on how the cables will need to be run. But if you can do it relatively easily (particularly if you're having other electrical work done), speakers in the kitchen or out on the patios can be an affordable attention getter. Also, the wireless speaker technology is getting better and better all the time. Since you'll have music playing whenever the house is being shown (see "Open-House Checklist" at the end of Step 5), prospective buyers won't be able to miss this great little feature.

12. *Closet organizer.* We get "closet envy" every time we visit a home with a remodeled closet. There's just something magical about all of those wooden hangers perfectly lined up in a row, the cabinet drawers filled with neatly folded socks.

Installing a closet organizer presents the perfect combination of practicality and indulgence. On one hand it will actually organize your closet, maximizing your storage space. On the other hand, many people dream of an organized closet. Since most master closets are pretty much the same, it's really easy for buyers to imagine transferring their current closet into this marvel of modern domestic engineering. Helping buyers imagine unpacking their clothes into a classy and uncluttered master closet is a great way to start transforming those daydreams into dollars.

Of course, these and any other possible improvements you might consider will cost money (and sometimes *lots* of money). Before you consider any home improvement project, it's worth taking a moment to think about your potential ROI.

What's Your ROI IQ?

As much as you will love to have new kitchens and bathrooms (and closets!), you probably can't avoid thinking about how much those renovations cost and what value—if any—you're likely to reclaim from those improvements when you sell. Luckily, there's a source out there that can tell you just how valuable those renovations may be at resale. *Remodeling* magazine publishes its annual "Cost vs. Value Report" comparing the average costs of several home renovations and the resale values of those improvements. The data are collected from sixty U.S. cities and cover a variety of projects from bathroom and deck additions to roof replacement and major kitchen remodels. A recent survey shows upscale siding replacement and midrange bathroom remodeling (about $10,000) to return over 100 percent on your investment. At the bottom of the list are sunrooms and home office remodels (although staging a nursery or extra room so that buyers could imagine it as a home office can really pay off).

Obviously, there's a lot of variation in the specific ROI you should expect for any renovation. The outcome for you depends heavily on your particular house, your neighborhood, the current market, and many other factors. The "Cost vs. Value Report" is most useful as a general guideline to help you decide which projects you want to do. You can view the latest results at www .remodeling.hw.net. It's important to remember that these data are coming from the remodeling industry, which obviously has an interest in convincing you that you'll get a great return on any work you have done. Also, it's important to note that these statistics assume that you'll sell within a year of renovating. And even that time frame may be too long, since it's reasonable to assume that a renovation is just like a car, which starts losing value the moment you drive it off the lot. With renovations, it's likely that once the job is done, its value starts dropping. Keep in mind, though, that it's not wise to make your renovation decisions based on ROI alone. There are other important questions to consider, such as: Is it worth the stress and inconvenience? Will you personally get value or enjoyment from the improvement before you sell?

And before getting started with any renovation, you should talk with a local real estate agent and a few contractors to get specific advice for your home and your real estate market.

ROI Is in the Eye of the Buyer

You have to be very careful when interpreting all these data about potential return on investment for renovations. As we'll see in Step 5, the more personally tailored a design is to you, the less likely it is to have the broad appeal necessary to garner the top return. If you really want to do something quirky and unique, go for it. But understand that prospective buyers are not likely to value the improvement as much as you do, so your ROI for those renovations is likely to be significantly lower than the statistics would suggest. Here's a perfect example:

Donna: I absolutely love the Coen brothers, and one of my favorite movies of theirs is *The Big Lebowski*. You probably won't remember, but when the Dude takes the rug from the *other* Jeffrey Lebowski's mansion, the tile floor has a really cool pattern to it. Well, I just had to have that floor, so Shannon and I replaced my kitchen floor with vinyl tiles to match that floor.

Shannon: You should've seen us—it was like a scene from *The Three Stooges*. Mom ended up gluing her glasses to her head and I glued my socks to my feet. But in the end, the floor looked great.

Donna: And I love that floor, not just because of the *Lebowski* connection but because we installed it ourselves. But I understand that nobody else is likely to love that floor as much as I do. In fact, some people might think it's hideous, and I can hardly blame them. So I really don't expect to get my money back on that floor, and I'll probably even replace it when it comes time to sell my house.

FOOL'S FABLE

What Do Buyers Want?

To maximize the potential appeal to buyers of any improvements you do, keep things as mainstream and timeless as possible. For specific ideas on what buyers are looking for, go to local open houses to see what gets people's attention and to get a sense of what the common amenities are in comparable homes in your area.

Another strategy is to uncover emerging trends. You can get a sense of "the next big thing" from the American Institute of Architects (AIA), which conducts an annual survey to determine what kind of work architects' clients are hiring them to do. Bathrooms and kitchens are perennial favorites, but there has been a recent trend for architects to design outdoor spaces (see "Staging the Outdoors" in Step 5 for suggestions on how to improve your outdoor space). These trends can help you understand exactly what current buyers will find most interesting. Visit the AIA Web site at www.aia.org/econ_designsurvey_results for more information.

FINANCING YOUR FIX-UP

It's usually the buyers who are the most focused on financing during a home transaction, but if you're financing repairs and renovations, you should understand the fundamentals as well.

Basically there are two types of loans to consider when financing your remodel or repair: a home equity line of credit (HELOC) or a fixed-rate second mortgage. A HELOC essentially works like a big credit card. You draw funds out of the account as you need them. As with credit cards, HELOCs are relatively easy to get, and there are no closing costs. The downside is that they have a variable interest rate.

A fixed-rate second mortgage works like a car loan. You get a big lump sum right away and you have a constant monthly payment throughout the life of the loan. The downside to a fixed-rate second mortgage is that they tend to have substantial closing costs added in up front.

So which financing option is right for you? You should definitely talk to a few lending institutions and discuss your options, but the general rule is if you're on a fixed budget and you're going to be spending the money right now (for example, to pay a contractor for the entire job), you'll probably be better off getting a fixed second to get the security of a fixed interest rate. If you're going to be doing lots of different projects over the next several months, or you're not sure how much you'll need, the flexibility of a HELOC will probably be better suited to your needs. You may also want to take interest rate trends into account. If rates clearly appear to be rising, a fixed-rate second might end up costing you less in the long term (and conversely, if rates are falling a HELOC might end up being cheaper). Once again, these are questions to ask lenders when you're shopping around for the right loan.

Keep Your Investment Low

One way to improve the return on your renovation investment is to keep the investment part of the equation as low as possible. There are two ways you could do this: get the work done for little money or get the best rate on your home improvement loan.

Don't Get Cheap

Trying to do any home project on the cheap is a risky proposition—we refer to it as "stepping over the dimes to pick up the nickels"—and we don't recommend it. That means you might pocket a little money now by spending less, but most likely it will cost you more in the long run. What usually happens is that homeowners hire the cheapest person they can find, figuring what's the point of sinking any more money into the house they're about to sell than they absolutely have to? Hiring the cheapest person increases your risk of poor workmanship or missed deadlines, both of which can cost you real money when you're ready to sell. We recommend that you get referrals from friends, check at least three or four estimates, and pick one from the middle of the pack (after all, you shouldn't overpay either).

Shannon: I know a certain woman who shall remain nameless (here's a hint: she's a real estate agent, loves her dog, and has a fabulous daughter) who was recently guilty of stepping over the dimes to pick up the nickels.

Donna: Gee, I wonder whom you could be talking about. Well, go on, tell them what I . . . I mean, what this *other* foolish woman did.

Shannon: Well, this completely anonymous woman—who needs to eventually sell her home for a lot of money so her daughter can retire to Hawaii—did a pretty substantial renovation on an underutilized room in her house. But she tried to save a few bucks on the sink and bought one of those cheap plastic utility sinks. That sink totally overshadows all of the other positive aspects of the room, and I just know that she would've added to the overall value of the house if she had installed a higher-end sink.

Donna: Something tells me that she will upgrade the sink before she sells. And, by the way, I highly doubt the daughter will end up in Hawaii, but she can visit her mother on Grand Cayman whenever she wants to.

DIY or Not?

Without a doubt the best way to save money on renovations is to do them yourself. Of course, most of us have neither the time nor the skills to take on any big projects. But, if you're feeling particularly ambitious, there's a Web site that can help you decide if doing it yourself will be worth your time, effort, and possible mental anguish. There's a wonderful service called "DIY or Not," which you can access from sources such as the Real Estate section of the *Los Angeles Times* Web site. Go to www.latimes.com and click on Real Estate and then Tools for Sellers on the left-hand side. From the next page, click on Do It Yourself . . . or Not? Then you can compare the cost of hiring someone or doing it yourself for many common renovation and repair projects. When you compare that information with the ROI statistics you got from

Remodeling magazine, you can see how a little DIY can go a long way.

Just make sure to be completely realistic and honest with yourself before launching into any DIY project. Do you really know what you're doing? And what are the possible consequences if you make a mistake? Remember, don't let emotions get in the way, and don't allow your pride to get between you and a successful sale. Sometimes even the handiest of handymen (or women) call in the pros.

Get the Best Loan Rate

The other way to keep your renovation costs down is to get the best possible rate on your loan. Besides shopping around, the most important thing you can do to get a lower rate is to raise your credit score.

When you're buying a home, you are acutely aware of your credit score and how it affects the interest rate on your mortgage. But as a seller you need to remember that your credit score also affects the rate on your HELOC or fixed second, which can dramatically impact how much your renovations or repairs actually cost.

Your credit score is simply a number that summarizes your credit history, so that lenders can easily determine whether to lend to you, and at what rate. While there are hundreds of different credit scores out there, the one most commonly used by banks and other lending institutions is the FICO (for Fair Isaac Corporation) score.

It's important to realize that the only credit score that matters to a potential lender is the one that they use, and since FICO is the most commonly accepted, it's the one that matters most. We've had clients find higher credit scores online, but that score is useless if the client's bank doesn't accept it.

Know the Score

What Determines Your FICO Score?

FICO scores range from 300 to 850, and while the exact method of determining the score is proprietary, scores are generally based on your payment history, outstanding debt, the length of your credit history, and inquiries made on your credit report (which lenders assume indicates an interest in taking on more debt). Keep in mind that only inquiries made within the past year affect your score, and lenders don't see every type of inquiry on your credit report. For example, future creditors will not see that you've checked your own report, which you should definitely do to review for any inaccuracies.

How Can You Improve Your Score?

Obviously, the most important factor in ensuring a good FICO score is a clean credit history. While you can't erase past problems—unless there are errors in your report (see below)—the longer you can maintain a clean credit record the better off you'll be. So just be sure to keep making every payment on time.

The one thing you can do right now is to pay off as much of your debt as possible. We recommend that you pay down any balances to half of the available credit. If you can pay off more, do so, and if you can pay them off completely, that's great (although keeping a small balance may actually be a bit better for your score). But don't close any accounts once you've paid them off. The more open accounts you have with zero balances, the better your score will be. Also, if you can increase your credit limits, that will instantly lower the percentage of credit being used, even without paying down your balance.

Finally, and we can't stress this enough, *check your credit reports*. Credit reports are notoriously error prone. It is your right and responsibility to check your own credit reports to make sure everything is accurate. Federal law mandates that you be provided with one free credit report from each of the three major credit bureaus every year. To get your report, go to www.annualcreditreport.com or call 1-877-322-8228.

REPAIR

Every house has things that need fixing, and even brand-new homes can have significant problems. But which problems do you need to fix before putting your house on the market?

Sometimes it is wiser to fix everything ahead of time. But not necessarily all the time. There are certain things that some buyers might rather receive a credit for and then fix themselves. They might be concerned that you didn't have it done properly (after all, you are about to move out), or they might have a personal preference for a certain style of replacement. Credits tend to work best for larger projects. For example, if you need a new air conditioner, you may want to hold off on replacing it and be prepared to offer the buyer a credit toward a new one (it's possible they won't ask for it), since they may want a top-of-the-line, high-efficiency model. Or, if your roof needs replacing, but doesn't look too bad from the ground, you could offer a credit to the buyers. If you replace it yourself, the buyers might be wary of the quality of the new roof, and they may be disappointed because they wanted to completely change the style of roof. You should discuss specific issues with your agent to determine the best strategy for you.

Inspect Yourself

The best way to determine your fix list is to have a home inspection. The inspector will tell you exactly what needs fixing, and you can go through the list with your agent and determine what is a "must-fix" and what isn't. Before we open up that can of worms, remember that you won't be able to get away with anything. Nothing will be overlooked, so you'll either have to repair it or disclose it. We're not saying that to scare you but to make sure you understand that you're not just fixing up your house to maximize the sale price—you're also doing it to protect yourself legally.

If you're planning to have a prelisting inspection, do it *before* you do any remodeling or staging. If the inspector finds anything significant, you don't want to damage newly painted walls, rip out new carpet, and so forth.

NO-BRAINER

Home inspections can be intimidating, like having an accountant scrutinize your personal finances or taking a good, long look at yourself in the mirror. To help alleviate the anxiety about home inspections, we sat down with a local inspector whom we have recommended to our clients for years. Hopefully he can answer many of your questions about inspections, and make your own inspection as comfortable and productive as possible. (See "Words from the Wise: The Inspector" on page 120.)

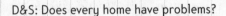

The Inspector

We encourage many of our sellers to have home inspections, particularly those who don't have a good sense of what condition their homes are really in. Obviously, an inspection is very useful in catching any big issues that might arise later, but it's just as important to take care of the little things that inspectors will inevitably find. That way, the prospective buyers don't feel like there are a thousand little things they'll have to fix if they decide to buy.

Paul Ferguson is a home inspector with Sherlock Home Inspections in Manhattan Beach, California. Paul has been doing home inspections since 1998. Before that he was a home builder, so he knows houses inside and out.

D&S: Our first question would have to be, What exactly is it that inspectors do?

Paul: We look at the six major areas of a house: foundation, structure, roof, electrical, plumbing, and heating. We determine what's working, what's not working, what needs fixing now, and what's going to need to be fixed in the not-too-distant future. When I'm done with the inspection, I sit down with the clients and do a complete verbal review of everything I found. I tell them how serious each issue is and whether it needs to be addressed immediately.

D&S: Does every home have problems?

Paul: I've never inspected a home without issues. There's always something that comes up, even in new homes. In fact, given how everything is subcontracted out these days, new homes actually have more issues than many older homes. I just inspected a house where the garbage disposal wasn't hooked up because the electrician and the plumber never coordinated to get it done.

D&S: We've seen inspection results that end up costing homeowners a ton of money or scuttling a deal. We were really surprised to find out that there's little government control over an industry that can have such an impact.

Paul: That's true. California has no state license requirement for home inspectors. Other states, like Massachusetts, do have government boards that regulate the industry. Either way, it's important to realize how imperative the home inspection is to the selling process, and to find a good, reputable inspector.

D&S: How do people do that?

Paul: The best way is always by referral from someone you trust. Ask your real estate agent or a friend who bought a home recently. You can also go to www.servicemagic

.com and submit a request for inspectors to contact you.

D&S: And what happens when something needs fixing? Will you fix it?

Paul: Federal law actually prohibits inspectors from doing any work on houses they've inspected within the last year. There's obviously the potential for a huge conflict of interest, so I'll point out the problem and tell them what kind of person they need to contact to get it fixed. I always tell clients to get three or four estimates for any work they need to have done. I also recommend that they avoid the lowest and the highest bids. The highest bidder probably doesn't want to do the job, and the lowest bidder probably won't do it right. Also, if something doesn't need fixing right away but is the kind of thing that requires regular maintenance, I'll point that out in the inspection just so the client knows about it and won't be surprised down the road.

D&S: So, do you recommend that sellers fix problems ahead of time?

Paul: That's a tricky one. Sellers are obligated to disclose the results of an inspection to the buyer. When the seller fixes something that the inspector found ahead of time, the buyer needs to know that it was fixed properly and not done on the cheap because the seller was about to move out. If sellers do fix things, I highly recommend that they have a follow-up inspection to document that the job was done properly. That way, there's no uncertainty on the buyer's part and they can be comfortable with the fix.

D&S: If sellers decide not to have an inspection, are there common problems they can look for and correct?

Paul: Here's are my list of top ten simple fixes that sellers can do:

1. Make sure your water heater isn't leaking and rusted. Set the water at or below $120°$ F.

2. Take a long, hard look at the roof and make sure it's completely intact.

3. Check for mold and mildew, especially near bathrooms and other wet spots. Whether you see it or not, if it's there you can be sure the buyer's inspector will find it. Mold really worries buyers, so if you suspect you have it you should definitely disclose it and you might even consider testing for it and getting it removed. If you go to www.servicemagic.com and search on Mold you'll be able to get specialists to test for mold and take care of any problems. Mold is a hot topic these days, so make sure you get more than one opinion if you think you do have a mold issue.

continued

WORDS FROM THE WISE

4. Check under every sink for leaks. A leak could be caused by a clogged trap in the drain (see "Destinking the Sinks" in Step 5).

5. Replace any burned-out lightbulbs. This is important because when inspectors find burned-out bulbs, we're not sure if it's the bulb or the switch. With everything else on the buyer's mind, you don't need to add this uncertainty.

6. Make sure all the doors have working doorstops. This is a cheap fix but can cause hundreds of dollars of damage when the doorknob goes through the wall.

7. If you've done custom work to your house, like taking off railings or fireplace screens, make sure you put them back.

8. Make sure your windows open and close easily. The guideline is that a child needs to be able to open the window with one hand in case of a fire. Also, make sure sliding doors slide smoothly. Do not use WD-40 for these things. The WD stands for "water displacement," which means that it's great for loosening rusted bolts or cleaning lawn mower blades, but it is not a lubricant. It might loosen things up at first, but eventually you'll have no grease in there and it'll just be metal on metal. Use silicone spray or graphite grease spray instead.

9. If you've got ceiling fans, they shouldn't wobble. You can buy a balancing kit and fix that problem.

10. For newer automatic garage doors, make sure the safety reverse works. Most people think that the optical sensor that stops the door also serves as a safety reverse. It doesn't. When I check a garage door, I hold my arm under it as it closes. It should stop and then go back up. If it doesn't stop, check on the light box of the opener. There should be two screws, one labeled "upward pressure" and the other "downward pressure." Just decrease the downward pressure until the door stops.

WORDS FROM THE WISE

Your Must-Fix List

Deciding what is a must-fix is completely subjective and is determined by your budget, your goals, and the amount of time and energy you can dedicate to the tasks. Basically, though, you want to rank the items that need fixing based on how obvious they'll be to prospective buyers. Broken windows, missing shingles, dripping sinks, or burned-out lightbulbs on the front porch all go high atop the list; a dead outlet in the garage or a sticky door in the basement would go much lower down. Paul had his own must-fix list, but we thought we'd add in our ideas. Here are a few common fixes that top many sellers' must-fix lists.

WD-40 is not a lubricant. Use silicone spray or graphite grease on sticky hinges, sliding doors, or locks.

INSIDER SECRET

Leaky Faucets   As Paul noted, this is high on the list of fixes, and that's because plumbing problems cause buyers' imaginations to run wild. Even though the leak may be insignificant, they imagine the nightmare of plumbers' shutting off the water, tearing out walls, and discovering a labyrinth of decrepit pipes like something out of *The Matrix*. Or they picture themselves trying to sleep at night with that faucet's drip . . . drip . . . drip echoing around in their brains. You get the point.

While there are many different types of faucets, most of them work on the same basic principles. When you turn the water on, you are opening a valve between a hard rubber washer and a sort of socket that it fits into called a seat. In the vast majority of cases, the leak is caused by a malfunction in that valve, either from the washer wearing away or from its not sealing perfectly in the seat. To fix a leak, you need to replace either the washer or the seat (or possibly both). If the seat cannot be removed, you can usually fix the problem by smoothing it out with something called a "seat-dressing tool."

For exact instructions, and to get the proper tools for the job, your best bet is to write down the brand of faucet you have and go to Lowe's or Home Depot. Both stores stock all the parts for just about every brand of faucet, and their employees can give you basic instructions for fixing the leak. As with every home improvement project, there are a few key points to keep in mind:

Don't forget to turn off the water to the faucet. We know it sounds obvious, but we've all made that mistake at some point. You'll most likely find shutoff valves down low on the wall behind the sink. If you don't see valves there, you'll need to work back along the line, shutting off valves as you find them and testing to see if the water stops running. You could also shut off the main water line to your house, which might be a bit more inconvenient but gets the job done. After you shut off the water, open the valves on the faucet to drain them completely.

If you have a two-handle faucet that is dripping, you can determine which one is the culprit by shutting off the water to either the hot or the cold side. If the leak stops, that's the leaky side. If the leak doesn't stop, turn the first side back on and shut off the other side. The dripping should stop, confirming that the leak is in that side.

If you are replacing any parts to the faucet, be sure to close the drain stopper to prevent anything from falling down the drain.

If you need to use pliers to unscrew anything, wrap the jaws with tape so they don't chew up the finish.

Before you turn the water back on, remove the aerator from the faucet spout. Don't know what an aerator is? No problem. Simply unscrew the cap over the water outlet and check that there is a fine mesh screen inside. If you don't remove this, it could get clogged when you turn the water back on.

When you're done, open the valves on the faucet first, then turn the water back on and let it flow until all the air is out of the system. Turn the water off and replace the aerator.

Of course, if your faucets are even a little bit old, it's probably a better idea to just replace them altogether. Faucets these days are easy to install and can dress up a bathroom for just a few dollars.

Running Toilets   When you flush the toilet, do you unconsciously jiggle the handle to make sure it fills properly? Do you no longer even notice that every five minutes the water in the toilet runs to keep the tank full? Buyers will definitely notice and that running water is the sound of dollars being subtracted from the sale price and flowing down the drain. Fixing toilets is so simple and inexpensive that you should probably up-grade all of your toilets while you're at it.

When you're doing toilet repairs, it is wise to empty the water tank before beginning. To do this, turn off the water to the toilet, flush the toilet, and then dry up the remaining water in the tank with a sponge or towel.

NO-BRAINER

Any major hardware store will sell just about every part you'll need to repair the toilet. The directions that come with each part are pretty self-explanatory, although for more details you may want to consult a home repair guide (see Recommended Reading). The most likely culprits are:

- *The stopper,* which is pulled up when you flush to release the water in the tank and then closes to allow the tank to refill. A running toilet is probably caused by a faulty stopper, which either isn't closing properly or is not completely sealed where it connects to the bottom of the tank.

- *The float mechanism,* which gauges the water level and automatically shuts off the water flow when the water reaches a certain level. If the float ball fills with water or gets stuck, the water won't be shut off properly.

- *The handle and chain,* which pull up the stopper, allowing the tank to empty. If the chain gets tangled or is set too tight, the stopper won't be able to close properly and water will leak out of the tank.

Caulking Around Tubs and Sinks   This is a great little fix that you can do in just a few minutes, but which can dramatically improve the look of your bathrooms. If you have old caulk around the tubs and sinks in your house, odds are it is peeling and black with dirt or mildew.

1. First, clean up the caulked joints. Mix about a half-gallon of warm water with about a half cup of bleach. Wearing rubber gloves, scrub the caulked joints with a sponge soaked in the bleach solution. Rinse with clean water and allow to dry completely.

2. If the caulk is still dirty, severely peeling, or if it's been over-applied and is very thick and uneven, carefully scrape it out using a flathead screwdriver. Wipe with a cloth dipped in rubbing alcohol and allow to dry.

3. If you're caulking around a tub, fill the tub with water before recaulking. Otherwise, if the caulk sets while the tub is empty, it may stretch and crack when the tub is eventually filled.

4. Apply a generous bead of caulk completely around the joint where the tub meets the walls or floor, or where the sink meets the countertop. Smooth the bead of caulk using a wet finger.

By the way, this technique for applying caulk also works for filling cracks between walls and trim, along internal corners where two walls meet, and around window and door frames.

Be sure to use the correct caulk for the job. This might seem ridiculously simple, but we know plenty of people who have made this mistake. Use watertight, silicone tub and tile caulk for bathrooms and latex, paintable caulk for filling cracks between painted surfaces.

NO-BRAINER

Nail Holes in the Walls   As we'll see in Step 5, properly staging your house for the market requires removing much—or even *all*—of your personal presence from the house. This often means removing personal photos and other pictures hanging throughout the house, leaving behind a wall potentially riddled with nail holes. You've got to fill those. Luckily, it's a relatively quick and easy process.

1. Using a small putty knife, apply enough joint compound to fill the hole, holding the knife at a low angle to the wall. Raising the angle of the knife, scrape away the excess. Allow the joint compound to dry completely.

2. Sand the surface smooth using fine grade (150 grit or so) sand-paper. Or, if your wall is not perfectly smooth, use a damp sanding sponge, which will leave the patch closer in texture to the surrounding wall.

3. Prime and paint the patched area.

Missing Baseboard Trim   The first few times we noticed a missing piece of baseboard trim in a house, we didn't think anything of it. After a dozen or so times, we began to think there were strange things afoot. Now, we've seen so many instances of missing trim pieces that we hardly even notice it anymore. Take a look around your house; the odds are pretty good that there's a piece of baseboard missing completely, or a piece that was re-placed and never painted, or some other oddity. It's as if there's a little baseboard gnome that goes from house to house and steals just a foot or two of trim from every house it visits.

All we can say is if you've got missing, damaged, or unfinished baseboard trim, be sure to fix it before the house goes on the market.

Stains on Walls   If you have fingerprints, smudges, or other common stains on your walls, repainting is a pretty straightforward process. For complete instructions, we recommend that you purchase a general home repair book such as *Home Depot Home Improvement 1-2-3* or *Lowe's Complete Home Improvement and Repair.* But there are two types of stains that exhibit the miraculous property of immediately bleeding through new paint:

1.   *Crayons, Ink, and Grease.* If you've got kids, you've probably got these stains somewhere in your house.

2.   *Water Stains.* If you've got water stains, you absolutely must determine if they are active or inactive. Basically, did the stains come from a onetime water occurrence, or do you have an ongoing leak? You need to find this out because if the leak is ongoing not only will any painting need to be redone, but when the buyers eventually discover the leak you could get sued for not disclosing it. If the water stain is not growing and it feels completely dry to the touch (a stain from an active leak might actually feel more cold than wet, but it's still a problem), it's probably safe to paint.

With these two types of stains you need to apply a primer/sealer rather than just standard primer. We prefer Kilz, which is available at most hardware stores and does a great job sealing away stains with just one coat. Be careful if you're just doing touch-up painting, as an undercoating of primer/sealer will make the painted area look different from the rest of the wall or ceiling. Your best bet is just to prime and paint the entire wall to ensure a uniform look.

Sliding Doors That Stick   Is there anyone out there who doesn't have a sliding screen door that sticks, rattles along its tracks, or jams up completely? We sure do.

Donna: Shannon, you have a little experience with sliders. Why don't you field this one?

Shannon: My mother is being a bit sarcastic, because I used to have the sliding screen door from hell, and I didn't even realize it. Every time I would open the screen door to go outside, it would jump off the track. And every time I would catch it and wrestle it back into place. I didn't even know I was doing it until I finally broke down and replaced the darn thing. I was stunned to discover just how wonderfully smooth and quiet a sliding screen door could actually be.

Donna: I told her all along how easy they are to replace. Just measure your current one (the standard sizes are either three or four feet wide, and there are a few heights to choose from) and buy a replacement at Lowe's or Home Depot. Follow the installation instructions and you should have the new doors up and running in less than an hour. If you think your old door can be salvaged, spray the track with silicone spray and slide the door back and forth a few times to lubricate the wheels.

This list of fixes is probably nothing compared to your own. Ultimately, though, you need to decide what is a must-fix for you. Remember, each little fix adds a few bricks to the stack and makes your house a bit more appealing. But if you just don't want to take the time or spend the money, there are many things you could leave as is. If you're not sure, ask yourself if this problem would bother you if you were a buyer. If the answer is yes, then you should seriously consider fixing it. If it's no, let it go.

The Fix That Isn't Fixed

Just because you've fixed something doesn't mean that it will appear fixed to a buyer. In fact, there are some "fixes" that can actually work against you. If something looks like it's been fixed haphazardly—like wallpaper that's been glued back in place or a patch on the ceiling that looks like a relief map of the Rocky Mountains—it will raise a buyer's suspicion. Not only will buyers wonder about that particular fix, but they'll assume there are many more shoddy fixes throughout the house. Basically, you want to make sure that any and all fixes look professionally done. When we go through a house, we can tell immediately if an overly ambitious handyman lives there, and buyers will pick up on that, too.

The best way to make things look professional is to hire a professional. Not only will that help you avoid the appearance of poor quality work, but it will protect you in the future as well. Make sure that any repairs that require permits actually have permits, and hire licensed professionals who offer guarantees for their work.

RENEW

As we mentioned earlier, an overwhelming majority of buyers would prefer to buy a new house rather than a lived-in one. Since it's impossible to make your house new again, we'll focus on what you can do to make it *appear* new.

That Not-Lived-In Look

Think back to when you first moved into an empty house, or when you bought a new bookcase or refrigerator. It was as if you had a blank canvas—a clean slate if you will—and you could position everything in its place perfectly. Let's use the refrigerator as an example. You open the door for the first time and it's beautifully white and cavernous inside. You begin loading it up, with drinks neatly arranged on the top shelf, Tupperware perfectly sorted below, condiments tucked into the door, and vegetables and meats in their proper drawers. When you finished, you should have taken a moment to appreciate the perfection of it, because the moment you close that door it's all over. Within days it's as if a cyclone tore through that fridge. There are stains everywhere; something noxious is dripping from the vegetable crisper; every cubic inch of space is packed with various soggy products and decomposing leftovers. You can hardly remember what it looked like only days before, and you can't imagine that you'll ever get it back to that pristine state. Well, that's just what we're going to do.

Whether it's your refrigerator, bookshelves, kitchen table, medicine cabinet, or filing cabinet, we've got a plan of attack to help you get back to the good old days when those things were brand new and life was grand. We like to call it our CCR technique:

Clear everything out.

Clean it all up.

Replace everything neatly.

It's a very simple technique. You want to go through your house room by room, focusing on each storage space and every horizontal surface that has anything on it. The first step is "Clear everything out." So if it's a bookcase, take every book off the shelves. If it's a kitchen table that doubles as a filing cabinet, remove every scrap of paper. Next, go through the pile and aggressively weed out everything that you don't want to keep. If there's any doubt about particular items, apply Donna and Shannon's Clutter Calculator (see page 132) to determine whether you should keep it, donate it, or throw it away. See Step 5 for more specific advice about decluttering your house.

Once you've winnowed the inventory down to the bare essentials, it's time for the second step: "Clean it up." Get into the cabinets with a vacuum cleaner to remove all the dust, and then wipe them down with a rag and your favorite cleaning spray. Make sure every flat surface is cleaned to a shine with the appropriate surface cleaner.

Finally, tackle the third step—"Replace everything neatly"—but only if it actually belongs there. If it doesn't, find its appropriate place. Remember, you're striving to create the illusion of a model home, and model homeowners don't pay bills while eating a late-night cheesecake at the kitchen table. Arrange the books in some aesthetically pleasing way and make sure all the spines are aligned. Replenish your cupboards so elegantly that they would make Martha Stewart jealous. Remember, this is *not* how you live but how you sell. Hopefully your house will sell quickly so won't have to maintain the illusion for very long.

An additional advantage of all this cleaning is that when you actually begin packing things up and moving out, you've already cleared away much of your unwanted stuff, so the move becomes much easier.

Donna and Shannon's Clutter Calculator

We generally recommend that you completely clear off every surface in your house and only put back at most one or two items. This is not an easy task, and we've seen clients brought to the verge of tears trying to decide what to keep and what to remove. To help you make it through this difficult process, we've created a series of questions to determine if what you've got is decor or detritus.

1. *Is it part of a collection (Franklin Mint Collector's Plates, vegetables that look like Elvis, etc.)?*

YES: Store the entire collection in the basement, sell it on eBay, or bury it in the backyard. It doesn't matter how you do it, just get it out of the house.

NO: Continue to next question.

2. *Have you ever defended your possession and display of this item by saying, "But it might be worth something someday"?*

YES: Sorry to break the news, but it won't be worth anything. Ever. You'll make more money donating it to Goodwill and taking the tax write-off.

NO: Continue to the next question.

3. *Does this item have any furniture or other accessories dedicated to it, like curio cabinets or other storage pieces?*

YES: This is an example of "metaclutter," the phenomenon where clutter has its own clutter that goes along with it. Not only does this mean you're dedicating too much space to this item, but it also suggests a certain fanatical devotion to this item, which is also problematic (see "Are You Hooked On Your Home?" in Step 1).

NO: Continue to the next question.

4. *When you picture yourself back when the item really meant something to you, are you wearing bell-bottoms and a "Disco Rules" T-shirt?*

YES: When you get rid of this item, be sure to get rid of the bell-bottoms and the "Disco Rules" T-shirt also.

NO: Continue to next question.

5. *Have you ever dug this item out of the trash because someone else thought it belonged there?*

YES: They were probably right.

NO: Continue to next question.

6. *Suppose there were a fire in your house. Would you go out of your way to rescue this item?*

continued

YES: This item should either be in a safe deposit box, or you need to get out more often.

NO: Continue.

If you answered no to every question and you're still not sure if what you've got is trash or treasure, just remember our mantra: *If in doubt, throw it out!* This recommendation applies to absolutely everything in your house (except for your spouse, of course).

By the way, there's also a "Clothing Corollary" to help you determine if you should get rid of an article of clothing or not.

1. *Some things never come back in style.*

2. *If you're ever that skinny again you'll have earned yourself an entire new wardrobe.*

A Place for Your Stuff

We don't explicitly tell clients that they should throw certain items in the trash, but when all of the storage in the house is filled up, you need to start thinking about alternatives. If you simply cannot part with all of the stuff that clutters up your house, you should rent a storage space and keep everything there until you find a new house. Do *not* rent one of the storage "pods" that gets dropped off in your driveway and sits out there like a giant RV (speaking of RVs, you shouldn't have any of those in your driveway either). Then you can fill that storage space to the rafters with all of your prized possessions.

Renewal by Association

In some cases, just renewing part of something can create an overall impression of newness. The best example of this is cabinet

Hanging On Too Long

Sometimes, trying to make something new again is just a lost cause. For example, renewing something that is terribly out of style isn't worth your time or money. One client of ours had wallpaper in his bathroom. As we saw it, there were two problems. First, it was peeling up a bit at the corners. Second, and more important, wallpaper seemed horribly outdated in that house, so even the best wallpaper was not a great selling point. Despite our suggestion that he strip the wallpaper and paint the bathroom, he decided to keep the wallpaper and just glue up the corners where it was peeling. The end result was a room that looked outdated compared with the rest of the house.

Another place where we often see this behavior is the driveway. Over the years, many neighborhoods have moved from the typical black asphalt driveway to more aesthetic driveways of brick, paving stones, or other materials. For example, if every one in your neighborhood has a brick driveway, it's probably not worthwhile to reblacktop the driveway, which will then be brand new but will still look old. You should probably consider moving up to a more conforming material.

FOOL'S FABLE

hardware. Replacing your kitchen or bathroom cabinetry is a major undertaking, and even resurfacing them can be quite expensive. We've found that simply replacing the knobs and pulls can make a big difference for just a little money. Coupled with a serious cleaning of doors and drawer fronts, new hardware can create the impression of all new cabinetry. We've found the best selection of knobs and pulls to be at EXPO Design Center, a higher-end interior design store owned by Home Depot (see the Web site www.expo.com for locations).

The Deal Is in the Details

Don't forget all the little things throughout your house that may need renewing. They represent a great opportunity to dress up your house without spending a lot.

· Replace old switch plate and outlet covers (remember, get the white ones, not the almond, which can look dingy and yellowed). Just to be safe, shut off the power beforehand.

· Update bathroom accessories like toilet-paper holders and towel rods.

· Replace any old doorknobs, light fixtures, and even A/C registers.

· Make sure that every door that needs a doorstop has one, and replace any old ones.

These may all sound like little, insignificant upgrades, but each one adds a few more bricks to the stack and improves your chances of a successful sale.

Renew Accessories, Too

You shouldn't restrict your renewal efforts to the house itself and those items that will stay with the new owners. It's worth spending some time and energy renewing accessories that can improve the overall look and feel of the house. For example, if you're planning on buying new furniture, curtains, area rugs, artwork, or unattached lighting for your new house, you may want to purchase them now and install everything in your current house to create a look of newness for prospective buyers. If you're worried about any of your new items being damaged during the move, be sure to purchase insurance that will cover the replacement value of the item in case of damage (see "Words from the Wise: The Mover" in Step 7). Also, make it clear to your agent that all of those new items are not included in the sale of the house.

Here are a few additional tips to help you renew your existing furniture and appliances if they've got any dents, water spots, or other signs of age:

Interior Designer

Before you put the finishing touches on any remodels, repairs, or renewals, or before you begin staging your house for the market, you may want to consider talking to an interior designer. Or, in lieu of hiring your own designer, you could just chat with ours.

Judy Smith, owner of Creative Interiors, has been our interior designer for years. Judy is brutally honest, but we appreciate her candor because we know she has our best interests at heart. Sometimes, though, when she's feeling particularly ambitious, it's actually a little intimidating. After a few hours with Judy, we can appreciate how our clients feel after we finish our no-holds-barred staging consultations with them.

We sat down with Judy to talk about general rules of interior design that can be utilized by a variety of sellers regardless of their specific homes.

D&S: Okay, let's get down to it. What kind of general advice do you have for home-owners considering selling their homes?

Judy: It all starts with one word: paint. Repainting gives sellers the best bang for their buck, and can make any house look so much better. You need to be careful with colors [see below], but if you play it safe you really can't go wrong.

Next, get rid of the clutter. I'm sure you tell clients this all the time, but removing clutter is the most cost-efficient way to improve your home's value. You can't beat the price (it's easy, free, and you may even make money by selling or donating your old stuff) and it really makes a big difference in the look and feel of your house.

Sometimes, though, you can actually clear away too much stuff. For example, I visit a surprising number of houses with no coffee table in front of the couch in the TV room. Sure, it opens up the room, but it looks like something's missing, and it attracts attention for all the wrong reasons. You want the house to look comfortable and inviting. You don't want anything to stick out, either because it's a really intrusive, gaudy item or because it's something that should be there but isn't.

D&S: We tell clients that decorating is a lot like dressing up for a fancy party. You want the entire outfit to work as a whole, without any single element more prominent than the rest. When you're looking at a room, close your eyes, spin around once, and then stop and look at the room. Whichever element catches your eye first should be carefully considered. If it's the velvet painting of those dogs playing poker, get rid of it. If it's a corner of the room that's totally empty, a tall plant can soften the space and make the room more welcoming. Speaking of plants, are there any general rules for which plants to use?

Judy: Basically, if your house has a traditional decor, you want to use softer plants. In contemporary homes look for plants with larger leaves, or consider succulents. Orchids are elegant in any setting; just make sure the planter fits in with your decor. These rules are not written in stone. The most important thing is that everything looks as if it's thriving.

D&S: Okay, as you know too well, picking and coordinating colors is not our forte. What advice do you have to help people pick the right colors?

Judy: Generally speaking, the more monochromatic you go, the larger the space will appear. Of course, you risk making buyers snow-blind if everything in the room is the exact same color. Try to limit the variety of colors to just a few, and avoid wildly different colors for accessories like pillows, artwork, and lamps. Another useful way to go monochrome is to paint ceilings the same color as the walls, which I find can make the room appear larger. Unless the room is really dark and needs a light-colored ceiling to open it up a bit, using the same color as the walls can give a

sense that the ceiling is higher than it actually is, since the border between the walls and the ceiling is blurred. When it comes to paint colors, just stick with neutrals. Everything goes with them and it's easy to change things up with a few new pillows or accessories. You should avoid plain white, though, since it's kind of harsh and aggressive. You're better off with beige, taupe, or sand.

D&S: Do you have specific color recommendations?

Judy: You can't go wrong with Monroe Bisque from Benjamin Moore for the walls and Swiss Coffee for the trim, also from Benjamin Moore.

D&S: What if a seller absolutely can't stand those neutral colors and refuses to use them, regardless of how many times we've told them to avoid getting emotional with their house before selling?

Judy: By the way, I completely agree with you that sellers need to be unemotional when staging their houses. In fact, I'd suggest that anyone hiring an interior designer set their egos aside and allow their designer to be completely candid. I know that sometimes I come across as a bit aggressive, but I'm just being honest. That's my job. Getting back to idiosyncratic colors. If you simply must diverge from basic

WORDS FROM THE WISE

neutrals, I'd suggest that you check out a few different design magazines, such as *House Beautiful* or *Traditional Home,* and look for the most popular colors. Or, if you ask the folks at your local paint store they should know what the most commonly requested colors are. The point is, if you're going to use a nonneutral color, make sure it's something that prospective buyers are likely to have seen before. You don't want to give them any design surprises.

D&S: What about finishes for the paints? Just flat for the walls and semigloss for the trim?

Judy: Not exactly. I recommend that my clients avoid flat finishes for walls, and instead opt for the lowest sheen available. Benjamin Moore offers Eggshell and Aqua-Velvet finishes that work just great. They give the walls a soft glow that I find more appealing than flat. For trim, go with a satin finish. I only recommend high gloss if it fits in perfectly with the current interior.

D&S: You recommended Benjamin Moore paint, which is pretty pricey stuff. Do you have any suggestions for discount paints?

Judy: I'm sorry, but I just can't recommend that anyone skimp on paint. There is such a huge difference in quality between ex-

pensive and cheap paints, it's simply worth spending the extra money. The difference in total cost won't be that great, and since you'll probably need to use more of the cheap paint to get good coverage, the actual difference in cost is even less. And the benefits of using good paint are immediately noticeable. You get richer colors, more consistent coverage, and a more professional look. Buyers will appreciate it, and there's a good chance you'll easily recoup the difference in cost when you sell.

D&S: What lighting advice do you have for sellers?

Judy: Believe it or not, I think overlighting is as big a problem, if not a bigger one, than underlighting. If your home is too dark, you probably realize it and you have a good idea how to fix the problem. Start with maximizing the natural light, and then add lamps and fixtures as necessary. But if your house is too bright, you may not even notice it. I walk into some homes and they feel like hospitals, with that sharp glare from fluorescent bulbs everywhere.

D&S: How do you fix that problem?

Judy: First of all, make sure you use frosted bulbs, which soften the light and create a more welcoming feel. High-efficiency bulbs are great for your pocketbook but lousy for ambience. They last forever, so don't throw them away, but replace them for showings. Also, indirect light in the form of wall sconces can add a very elegant touch to any room. Finally, one little tip that most people overlook: light fixtures are not just supposed to look good themselves; they're supposed to make *you* look good. Don't just look up at the ceiling; look at the other people in your house. If they look all washed out, you need to soften up the lighting.

D&S: What's the best way for people to find an interior designer?

Judy: As with just about every other service provider, referrals are always best. Talk to your friends who have hired a designer (or whose houses look like they've been professionally designed, since they probably have) and ask them if they could recommend anyone. Also, you can submit a request for bids from multiple designers at ServiceMagic (www.servicemagic .com).

WORDS FROM THE WISE

- For water spots or rings on furniture, try rubbing a bit of toothpaste onto the stain with a damp cloth. As with any furniture or fabric fix, always test an inconspicuous area for color fastness.

- You can use a walnut to hide scratches on light-colored wooden furniture or flooring. Break the nut in half and rub the exposed meat over the scratch. The oil from the walnut makes the scratch less noticeable.

Painting

As our interior designer, Judy Smith, has mentioned (see "Words from the Wise:

If your interior designer doesn't challenge you occasionally, or present ideas that you disagree with, he or she is probably not being honest enough with you and you're not getting your money's worth.

INSIDER SECRET

Interior Designer" above), if you're willing to spend a few bucks to update your house before putting it on the market, having the interior repainted is one of the most cost-effective renewals you can do. The Web site HomeGain.com, which will do a quick customized analysis of your home's needs, estimates that your home is likely to increase in value almost $1.50 for every dollar you spend painting the interior.

Light fixtures aren't supposed to just look good; they're also supposed to make *you* look good.

NO-BRAINER

Another appealing aspect of painting is that it's something most of us can do ourselves. At the very least, you can touch up nail holes or stains around the house. Or, if you're feeling particularly ambitious, you can do the entire job.

Beyond the helpful tips found in our chat with the interior designer, here are a few more things you can do to help ensure that your paint job has the maximum positive impact.

Time It Right   If you're painting just before you sell, you're likely to hire someone on the cheap end of the spectrum. That's perfectly reasonable, but you absolutely must make sure they get the job done on time. And that means everything is finished at least a few days before any showings, allowing ample time to get rid of the paint smell. Car buyers might love "new car smell," but homebuyers do not feel the same way about "new paint smell."

Don't Skimp on Supplies   There's a reason why high-quality paints and brushes are expensive: they're worth it. Not only will the end result look more professional—with richer colors and a more consistent finish—but the application process will be easier and faster for the painter (that could be *you*). So spring for the Benjamin Moore or similar quality paint (you may even want to splurge on Benjamin Moore's high-end line, Aura, which is really amazing stuff), buy the

Don't forget to paint the kitchen, which can get coated in grease. Make sure to use a primer/sealer, and pay particularly close attention to the ceiling above the stove.

INSIDER SECRET

Wooster or Purdy brushes, and get a few drop cloths made of canvas rather than plastic. The nice thing about these high-quality supplies is that they'll last much longer than the cheaper versions, so they're likely to be more cost-efficient in the long run.

Custom Colors   One of the biggest problems homeowners have when painting themselves is deciding which colors to choose. We've talked about how keeping it neutral is the safest way to go (see "Words from the Wise: Interior Designer" on page 137 for specific color recommendations). If there's a particular color you've seen in a magazine or elsewhere, though, you can take the sample to the paint store and they'll match it as closely as possible.

If you do choose to use a nonneutral color make sure you keep an eye on the overall palette. We have had clients who went into every room and picked a color that they liked and the house looked like a box of crayons. Nothing was cohesive and it seemed choppy moving from room to room.

From Painting to Staging

One added benefit of painting the interior of your house is that preparing to paint is an excellent first step toward properly staging your house for the market. The painters will remove everything from the walls, take down light fixtures and switch plate covers, and either move all the furniture to the middle of the room or take it all out of the room. Consider asking the painters to leave everything where it is when they're done, so that you can pack up some things, donate or sell others, and put what's left back in its proper place.

And that leads us to the next step on the road to SOLD. In this next chapter we'll help you determine what needs to go and what can stay and also help you redecorate your home ("set the stage," if you will) to create the most appealing atmosphere possible.

5

Set the Stage to Sell

IT'S NOT THAT we're mean people. It's just that a big part of our job involves explaining to our clients, in excruciating detail, every last thing that they need to change about their homes before they sell. And it's not that we think our clients have bad taste, although we have seen more than our share of home decor train wrecks. It's just that *any* personal taste can get in the way of a successful sale. That's really the essence of staging, removing yourself from the picture so that prospective buyers can place themselves in the house. But before we get into the specifics of how to stage your house for sale, let's explore a bit further exactly what staging is.

We use the term *staging* just about every day, and while we have a pretty good sense of what it means, we realize that many people might not know exactly what we're talking about. Generally speaking, staging includes just about everything you do to prepare your house so it's ready to be shown. More specifically, your home should look, sound, smell, and feel perfectly clean, comfortable,

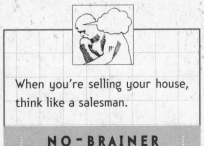

When you're selling your house, think like a salesman.

NO-BRAINER

and inviting to anyone who visits (see "Come to Your Senses" opposite). Think of it as creating an atmosphere such that when prospective buyers walk through the door they experience the sensation of coming home and not wanting to leave.

To get yourself ready to stage your house, you first need to get in the proper state of mind. This might sound ridiculously obvious, but when you're selling your house, you need to think like a salesperson or, more specifically, an advertiser. What you're really setting the stage for is a slick, sexy commercial just like those you see every day for beer or SUVs. As with those types of commercials, you're selling the fantasy of your house, not the reality. That's not to say you should ever be dishonest, but proper staging will present an image of your house that doesn't reflect the everyday reality of living there but instead shows an idealized version of how someone *could* live there, if only they would submit the winning offer—and quickly!

SUV ads show you gaggles of sturdy twentysomethings off-roading around the Grand Canyon. The reality is SUV drivers are much more likely to be caught in bumper-to-bumper traffic, paying a small fortune to fill up the tank every few days. It's the same with your average beer commercial. You'll never attract some Playmate or Chippendale just by ordering a Heineken, but it's obviously very appealing to think that it *could* happen.

When it comes to selling your house, the image you present will not be reality, but just look around at how many SUVs are on the road and how much beer gets sold. It works. For example, you'll stage your kitchen to create an image of the wonderful dinner parties that could be hosted there, with all the guests perfectly dressed and the conversation stimulating and sophisticated. You don't want to ever let potential buyers think about how that kitchen will look when the party's over and they have to clean up that huge mess.

Remember, as we said before, how you live in a house and how you sell it are two very different things. We can't imagine anyone living full time in a beer commercial and we can't imagine anyone keeping their home in perfectly staged condition as they live in it day after day (Donna gave up trying years ago). As we'll see in this chapter, there's potentially a huge amount of work involved in staging a house. But the better you stage, the fewer days your house is likely to be on the market, and the more likely it is to pay off in real dollars.

Come to Your Senses

Because your audience will be visiting your "stage" in person, you have the advantage of appealing to all their senses.

Sight

Obviously, you want your house to be visually appealing, and we've already talked a bit about how to do so. But in terms of staging, this means getting rid of all the clutter, clearing out some furniture to open things up, and removing anything ugly or unappealing.

Sound

Potential buyers are highly sensitive to unpleasant sounds, although silence can feel strange, too. Playing classical music on the stereo is very inviting, while using a fountain indoors or out can help diminish traffic noise. Jarring noises like old bathroom fans can be particularly bad, and plumbing noises can hint at significant problems. Do an audio inventory of your house and listen closely for any troublesome sounds.

continued

Smell

Many sellers completely overlook smell, which is an extremely powerful trigger of vivid memories. The problem is that most of us are so used to the smells in our homes, we don't even notice them (see "Does Your House Have House-itosis" on page 149). You must get an objective nose to walk through your house and tell you what stinks.

Touch

The sense of touch is not as directly utilized as the other senses, but it's still important. There's a famous woodworker in Southern California named Sam Maloof. One of the characteristics he strives for in his work is that it be "touchable," that it makes you want to slide your hand over its luxurious surface. Your home should feel "touchable," such that it draws people in and makes them want to immerse themselves in it. Make your living space accessible so that buyers sit down and stay for a while.

Taste

Okay, we're cheating a bit on this one. We're not really talking about tasting things in your house (although a batch of chocolate chip cookies always goes over well); we're talking about personal style. In this case, the more personal, the worse it is. Your house should be tasteful, with simple, subtle colors and an emphasis on clean. But as we'll see, you want to take yourself out of the picture (sometimes quite literally).

When all of that is taken together, it creates something we usually call ambience. We always have a tough time defining ambience for our clients, but it's kind of like pornography (without the negative connotation): you know it when you see it. If you appeal to all five senses, and follow the guidelines in this chapter, you'll create the perfect ambience for selling your home.

HOW MUCH STAGING IS ENOUGH?

To put it simply, you can never do too much to stage your house for the market. No matter how much you do, there's always something more that can be done. It's totally up to you to decide how much staging you can stand, but remember that every little extra touch you add stacks on a few more bricks on the pile and increases your chances of a successful sale.

No matter how thoroughly you stage your house, there's always more you can do.

NO-BRAINER

For most of us, though, our house under normal living conditions is so far from perfectly staged that we might not even know where to begin. One strategy we recommend to help you get started is to pick up an interior design magazine that matches the general decor of your house. As you flip through the magazine, rip out pages showing a kitchen, living room, bedroom, and bathroom. Then, stand at the entrance to those rooms in your house, hold up the picture, and compare the two scenes. Specifically, what do you see in your kitchen, bathroom, and other rooms that you don't see in the photos? Our guess is that you'll see lots of clutter, dirt, stains, and other obvious indications that your house is a place where people actually live, not the site of a photo shoot for some glossy magazine. There's no need to feel guilty or disappointed that your house is a mess, nor should you feel hopeless that you'll never get your house to look like those in the photos.

The purpose of this little exercise is simply to help you get a sense of where to focus your efforts when staging your house. Most likely, your major concerns will be clutter, dirt, and light. When you look at the magazine photos, there's usually minimal decor and no misplaced accent pieces. Everything is spotless, and the room is beautifully lit. As we continue along, keep those points in mind as you work to make your home as perfectly staged as possible.

CLEANING

Your goal here is simple: to get your house as immaculately clean as it's ever been. Keeping everything spotless while your house is on the market is probably the biggest challenge that sellers face, but it's also one of the most important. Buyers will viscerally sense whether a home is clean or not, and it will affect their perception of everything about your home (and their perception of you as well). You want to capture that feeling of walking into a ritzy hotel room, where everything is perfect and it lures you in and refreshes you almost instantly. "But wait," you say, "those hotels have an entire cleaning crew getting those rooms so perfect." Well, then you should, too. Maybe not a full-time crew that cleans your house daily, but you should hire a cleaning crew at least once to give your house a thorough scrubbing. These guys will find things to clean that you didn't even know you had. It's basically like "detailing" a car, except for your entire house.

Once the cleaning crew is finished, you'll wish you could open your house to buyers at that very moment. Unfortunately, you're faced with the daunting task of maintaining that level of clean for the entire time your house is on the market. It's not easy, but here are four suggestions to help you succeed.

I. From now on, clean your kitchen floor with a sponge rather than a mop. Yes, we know, that does mean getting down on your hands and knees and doing your best Cinderella impression.

2. You want your windows to be spotless, but obviously you're not going to wash all of them before each showing. Plan on washing all prominent windows and sliding doors once a week.

3. Replacing doormats doesn't just make your entrances look nicer, it also helps minimize the amount of dirt that gets tracked into your house.

4. Keep an eye out for trouble spots where dirt and dust tend to accumulate. Regularly vacuum in corners and along floorboards. Also check on either side of thresholds, where dirt often gets swept and can hide for years.

Does Your House Have House-itosis?

Sellers often underestimate the power of smells. You may not want to admit it, but your house stinks. Now, don't get too offended, everyone's house stinks in one way or another. It's kind of like bad breath, which hangs out literally right under your nose, and you don't even realize it. Somehow, we're immune to our own offensive odors. It's the same with your house. Since you live there all the time, you've just gotten so used to the smells that you don't even notice the variety of pungent, offensive aromas that we like to call "house-itosis."

Destinking your house is really a two-step process. First, you've got to find out what really smells. Have you ever walked into someone's house and immediately smelled that they had a dog? Or that they smoked? As hard as it is to believe, those people probably don't even notice the smells that you pick up the moment you walk through the door. And guess what? Most people who walk into your house can't believe that you don't notice the smells that hit them. You really need a virgin nose to do a smell analysis of your house and, most important, tell you exactly what stinks in nauseating detail.

Ask yourself, "How many people do I know who'll tell me that my breath stinks?" Probably not very many, but you need to find someone just as brutally honest to tell you that you've got house-itosis. A good real estate agent should do the job, but it certainly wouldn't hurt to get a second opinion from a close friend.

Now that you know what smells, what do you do about it? Obviously, there are thousands of possible smells that can infiltrate your house. We'll just tackle a few of the more common ones here.

Destinking the Sinks

Bathroom Sink   You may get used to certain smells in your house, like pet, cigarette, or baby smells, but you would have to be profoundly compromised nasally not to notice when you've got an evil stink demon living in your bathroom sink. It's not your fault, really. The mechanics of the bathroom sink drain are mostly to blame. Basically, the stopper is controlled by a metal rod stuck into the drain horizontally, which is connected up to the faucet allowing you to open and close the drain.

Now, imagine this scenario (if you've got a weak stomach, you may want to skip ahead): Every time you wash your face, shave, or brush your hair, lots of unpleasant biomatter flows down the drain, along with soap, shaving cream, and other various lotions and balms. Invariably, some of it gets stuck on that metal rod. After all, *it's sticking right out into the drain,* perfectly placed to capture whatever flows by. Eventually, that mass grows, begins to clog up the drain, and climbs up the base of the stopper. (How is it that we can have a satellite orbiting Jupiter and self-adhesive stamps, but we can't design a better sink stopper?) You pour Drano or some such product down there, and that only makes the clog angrier. Before you can stop it, the clog begins emitting a funk that would set James Brown's bootie a-shakin'. It's time to take serious action.

First of all, you've got to unclog the drain. To do this, you need to remove the stopper. Move it to the open position, and see if it will just lift out. Otherwise, you'll need to get under the sink and remove that horizontal rod, which is holding the stopper in place. To do this, simply unscrew the little cap on the back of the drain. While holding the stopper, slide that rod back and lift out the stopper. Be sure to replace the rod and rescrew the cap so water won't leak out while you're cleaning the drain. *Beware:* What you find clinging to the stopper might shock you. Next, clean off the stopper and clear the drain. A bottle-washing brush works perfectly for clearing sink drains. You want to make sure you get down to that elbow in the drain (the trap) and push everything through. Run plenty of hot water to flush the drain.

Now, it's time to tackle the smell. First, pour about a half gallon of bleach down the drain and let it sit for at least twenty minutes. Next, bring a teakettle of water to boil, and pour the very hot water down the drain. That should banish the beast. But beware. He'll be back. It's just a matter of time.

Kitchen Sink   Eliminating foul odors from the kitchen sink can be done with much the same technique as you employed in the bathroom. Additionally, if you have a garbage disposal, we recommend you grind a half lemon in there whenever your house will be shown. (And, by the way, don't just waste a half lemon down the drain. Juice the other half and combine in a cocktail shaker of ice with 2 tablespoons lime juice, 2 tablespoons sugar, and 2 cups water. Shake the ingredients together and pour into a tall glass. Garnish with a slice of lemon and you've got yourself an excellent lemonade. If you're feeling particularly stressed out, you can also add an ounce or two of whisky for a nice whisky sour.)

Pet Smells

Pet smells are the perfect example of how homeowners can get so accustomed to a rank aroma that they don't even notice it. It is so obvious to everyone else who walks through the door that there are pets in the house, and yet the owners are probably completely unaware of the smell. Basically, if you've got pets, regardless of how well behaved they are, assume you've got bad pet smells throughout your house. Don't get defensive; just get rid of the smell.

The most common problem for pet owners is urine on the carpet. The best way to find the offending spots is to turn off the lights and shine a black light on your carpets. If there are stains, you'll immediately see them as solid white spots.

If you haven't already done so, *do not* steam-clean the carpets, since the heat can actually bond the protein in the urine to the carpet fibers, thus setting the stain almost permanently. Also, avoid any strong-smelling cleaners, since they can encourage your pet to return and mark the spot with his own scent. Instead, try one of the enzyme cleaners—either liquids or powders— available at Petco and other pet stores. A favorite of ours is Nature's Miracle, which you just spray on the stain and allow to dry. The enzymes consume the stain and odor and when it all dries the smell is gone. Give yourself at least a couple of weeks to eliminate the smell completely, since it may take a while for the carpet to dry completely or you may need multiple applications.

For dog owners, make sure your pet gets shampooed just before your house goes on the market, and thoroughly clean (or replace) dog beds or other smelly accessories.

For cat owners, you should probably clean the litter box twice as often as usual, and consider getting a covered litter box.

For all pets, minimize pet food odors by placing food dishes in discreet locations and cleaning them out frequently.

Believe it or not, pet smells are probably covering your walls as well. If you are going to paint, use a primer/sealer such as Kilz which will help eliminate any odor.

Cooking Smells

Let's see, how can we put this delicately, without offending anyone? How about this: some foods just stink. It's completely subjective, but we can safely generalize that food smells that we find offensive will probably offend many other people as well. And for us, cabbage tops the list. Whether it's Hungarian stuffed cabbage, Korean kimchi, or German sauerkraut, the smell produced by cooked cabbage seems to linger for days. And it just plain stinks.

To be safe, avoid cooking particularly aromatic dishes up to a few days before showing the house. Thoroughly clean up afterward, store leftovers in airtight containers, and air out the kitchen as much as possible.

Also, be sure to clean or replace the filter in your stove exhaust, which is probably caked with grease and packed with the smells of a thousand odiferous dinners.

Smoke Smells

If you smoke you should think about quitting, if not for your health then at least for your bottom line. When nonsmoking buyers walk into a house that smells of smoke, they immediately assume the sellers are less than meticulous caretakers of the house. They'll adopt a much more skeptical mind-set as they walk through the house and start looking for other problems to find.

To get rid of the smoke smell, first stop smoking inside the house. Next, open up the windows and air out the entire house as much as possible. Beat couches and mattresses with your hand or a tennis racket. Finally, clean your carpet, sofas, mattresses, and every other offending item with a cleaning powder containing baking soda. Also think about having any draperies cleaned.

Must (a Must to Remove)

Musty smells are not just unpleasant; they also prompt buyers to immediately make the leap to mold. Even if you don't have any mold in your house, musty smells will send prospective buyers daydreaming about endless inspections and escalating fees for removal. As with electrical and plumbing issues, mold is a mystery to most buyers. And buyers approach mysteries with the assumption that what they don't know will cost them (big time). So if musty smells are a problem in your house, open the windows and air everything out as much as possible. You can also try putting small dishes of vinegar in particularly musty spots.

Baby Smells

While you may decide to board your dog during open houses, it's virtually impossible to remove all evidence of your baby's presence in the house. And when you're talking about baby smells, diapers are high atop the list.

If you don't already have a diaper disposal device, such as a Diaper Genie or Diaper Dekor, get one. Even if you have one, it's probably wise to clean it thoroughly and tuck it away in a closet. And while you're in the closet, make sure you've got a covered laundry hamper.

Oddly enough, even nice baby smells can be problematic. The perfumes on diapers and baby powders can create the sense that your house is one big nursery, which can be off-putting to people without children or those whose baby-rearing years are far behind or many years in front of them. Be sure to air out the baby's room and keep diapers and powders tucked away in a drawer.

The Sweet Smell of Success

Once you've removed all of the obviously objectionable odors, you may want to consider adding a few pleasant aromas to your house. While this may seem like a simple operation, it can be very risky. You may have favorite scents or potpourris that you've used for years and you hardly notice them, but they'll hit new visitors like a smack in the face. Scents are just like paint colors: you want to make sure they are neutral and inoffensive. Here are a few guidelines to help you add just the right aroma to your home:

Do not use anything that smells like fruit, flowers, spices, or vanilla.

Do not use any potpourri. Even if it's mildly aromatic, it's still just dead flowers.

Do use Glade Clean Linen–scented air fresheners in your bathrooms. Or go to the store and smell a sample of it to get a sense of the neutral aroma that we're talking about.

Do keep fresh flowers in the house. That's the only flowery scent allowed.

Do have a basket of fresh fruit in the kitchen and grind a half lemon in the garbage disposal. Those are the only fruity scents allowed.

DECLUTTERING

We introduced decluttering in the last chapter when we talked about "renewal" and how you should clear things out, clean them up, and replace them perfectly (the CCR technique). Generally speaking, clutter is the most common problem we encounter when staging a client's house. The problem with clutter is not just that it takes up space and makes your home look smaller, but much of it tends to have personal significance, preventing buyers from moving in mentally. In fact, we would even say that the more clutter you have, the more personal it tends to be, and the harder it is to get rid of. So it turns out that people who need to declutter the most have the hardest time doing so. That's why it's so important to have an honest relationship with your agent, so you can count on him or her to tell you the truth.

Decluttering simply means removing as much of your stuff as possible from the house, so that tables that should be empty are empty, coffee tables have just a few select items on them, and nothing appears out of place or crowded. As we'll see when we chat with our Feng Shui expert, creating an open, airy feeling to your home is the top priority. As simple as it may seem, decluttering is hardly easy for most of us. Besides your personal attachment to many items throughout your house, there's also the issue of where to store all that stuff and how to arrange what's left. Here are a few suggestions to make your decluttering chore more efficient and effective.

From Trash to Treasure

The Garage Sale   One of the most common ways that sellers clear out their homes is to have a yard sale. If the thought of laying out all your stuff to be sifted through by strangers makes you a little queasy, by all means skip ahead to the next section. But if you're planning on holding a garage sale to declutter your house (and possibly make some good money at the same time), here are some tips to make your day more pleasant and profitable:

1. *Advertise.* Place an ad in the local paper and post a listing on Craigslist (www.craigslist.com). These are the spots that the hardcore garage sale devotees will look.

2. *Post signs.* Make large, neatly written signs, and check the local regulations for posting so they're not immediately taken down.

3. Call your event a moving sale. Moving sales tend to hold greater appeal than garage sales because people assume there will be a wider variety of goods for sale.

4. Embrace the "early birds." As soon as you start setting up, they'll be there. So be ready for them, since early birds tend to be enthusiastic buyers.

5. Price everything to sell. While you do want to make some money, your primary goal is to get rid of everything.

6. Sell, sell, sell! Most people who go to garage sales don't have anything specific in mind. Convince them that what you've got is exactly what they want.

When you're done, box up whatever's left and take it to Goodwill (see "Give It Away" on page 158).

The Highest Bidder   Another option for selling your stuff is to auction it off through eBay. If you've never used eBay before, or if you're just an infrequent seller, here are some tips to help you become an online entrepreneur:

1. Always include a photograph with your auction. Regardless of what you're selling, buyers much prefer to see the product before bidding. This may be just the excuse to finally start using that digital camera.

2. Be professional. That means you should clearly state the shipping costs and make it as easy as possible for buyers to pay for items. Using PayPal or accepting credit cards will make your auction more appealing.

3. Do your research. Check out auctions for similar products to see how much they're selling for and to gauge the interest that's out there. Note what it is about some auctions (starting price, reserve price, etc.) that distinguishes auctions that close for high prices and those that close lower.

4. Work on your feedback ratings. Buyers want to see that you have a track record of positive transactions. If you're new to eBay, consider starting off by selling lower priced items and building up your positive feedback.

Give It Away   Instead of selling your old items through a garage sale or on eBay, you may want to donate them and take the tax deduction. This can be a relatively easy way to quickly declutter your house and lower your tax burden at the same time. In fact, many items may be worth more when you use them as a tax deduction than when you go to the trouble to sell them yourself. There are, of course, rules governing charitable donations of real goods. Here's a quick overview:

1. Deduct noncash charitable contributions. Noncash charitable contributions are only deductible if you itemize the deductions on your tax return. Since you own your home, it is most likely that you do itemize, so this should not be an issue.

2. Deduct fair market value. When you donate items to groups such as Goodwill, you can deduct the fair market value of those items. For old clothing, furniture, books, and similar items, the fair market value is the amount you could reasonably expect to get at a garage sale. Charitable organizations like Goodwill should be able to provide you with current fair market value for a variety of donated products.

3. Other considerations. If the total value for a single item or group of similar items is more than $500, you will need to complete IRS Form 8283, listing the items donated. If the total value is more than $5,000 you will probably need to have an appraisal done.

Don't Improvise Your Storage

Now that you've sold or donated everything you no longer want, it's time to turn your attention to everything that's left in the house. In some homes items that should be stored away begin to creep out into the house, setting up residence in places they don't belong. These things will be "stored" throughout the house for so long that they're no longer visible to the homeowners, and they actually become part of the decor. For example, stacking a decade's worth of *National Geographic* to create a giant yellow obelisk in the living room is neither storage nor sculpture. It's clutter, and it needs to go.

The most likely candidates for this kind of improvised storage are magazines, bills, and other semi-important paperwork. For many homeowners, just about any flat surface—particularly the kitchen table and countertops—can act as an impromptu filing cabinet. We recently visited a house in which the homeowner had installed a beautiful built-in wine cabinet, complete with a few rows of small cube-shaped shelves to hold wine bottles. While half of the spaces held bottles, the other half became a series of mail slots, holding bills, checks not yet cashed, and letters not yet mailed. Not good.

Another commonly used space for improvised storage is under the bed. If your bed has built-in cabinets underneath, that's one thing. If you're just stuffing anything under there that will fit, that's clutter. Even if you can't actually see under the bed, you should clear it out. It's kind of like vacuuming underneath your couches. You can't actually see that it's clean, but somehow the room just *feels* cleaner (see "Words from the Wise: The Feng Shui

Lady" on page 166 for a deeper mystical analysis of your home). We also find that homeowners sometimes use their outdoor space as improvised storage, and we're not just talking about the '71 Chevy up on blocks in the front yard. Even non-gearheads are sometimes guilty of stashing tools, building materials, and many other things on the back porch or in the yard. The biggest offenders are probably children's toys, bikes, and other multicolor monstrosities. When buyers see this, they assume that the house is busting at its seams and that there's just not enough space to accommodate a normal family.

Finally, we find that many homeowners use the top of the refrigerator for improvised storage. Parents, in particular, like to use this space to tuck things away and out of reach of the kids (or so they hope). We recently heard a story about a young couple that did just that, only to walk into the kitchen one day and find their three-year-old son sitting on top of the refrigerator. Since his parents had always hidden things from him up there, he thought the top of the fridge must be the most magical place on earth. After that, his parents kept the top of the refrigerator clear, and it's worth learning from their experience.

As we mentioned when we talked about children's toys, the biggest problem with these types of improvised storage spaces is that they create the impression that there's not enough real storage in the house, and that can really impede prospective buyers from moving in mentally.

Everything in Its Place

Besides creating storage space out of places not intended for storage, another way we create clutter is by not actively creating proper places for things to go. Remember that old saying "A place for everything and everything in its place." It's a nice thought but much easier said than done. Most of us live by the saying "Any place for anything, and wherever it is, that's its place." We just leave things wherever they fall, and that becomes their place. Over the years every square inch of the house becomes the place for something, and we find ourselves living with clutter without even realizing it.

Donna: When Shannon was little, she definitely lived that way. Her philosophy was "Wherever it lands, that's where it goes." You could barely open the door to her room, and inside there were vast snowdrifts of clothes, books, and papers, with a narrow path from the door to the bed and from the bed to the desk. She seemed happy, and she knew exactly where everything was, so I just shut the door and imagined that the room was clean.

Shannon: Gee, I wonder where I got my knack for tidiness. Mom always wanted a two-story house, not just for the extra space, but so that when she had guests over she could basically sweep up all the clutter from downstairs and throw it into an upstairs room. She always had a tactful way of deflecting requests for tours of the second floor, leaving guests to assume that the whole house was just as immaculate as the downstairs.

Donna: It worked for years, and I only cleaned up the second floor when I sold that house.

To declutter effectively, you need to define the appropriate place for everything. That means freeing up storage space, drawers, and shelves and specifically designating that as the place for something or a group of things. For example, we have a client who has a "magic drawer" in her house. What's magic about the drawer is that whenever she's looking for something, it's in the drawer. The trick is that she purposefully puts all the important things she's likely to lose (like her car keys, wallet, sunglasses, important bills, etc.) into that drawer. So rather than everything getting scattered around the house, and her searching all over the house

Resistance Is Futile

Some clients vehemently resist our calls to declutter. They usually say something like, "Whenever I clean up I can never find anything afterward." Or "Regardless of how chaotic things may look to the uninitiated, I know where everything is." Or, most ominous of all, "I have a system." Regardless of how true each of these statements may be, they describe how people *live* in their homes, not how they should *sell* them. What appears as a complex, perfectly organized system to you looks like the aftermath of a hurricane to a prospective buyer.

We sympathize with those of you who won't be able to find anything after you eventually clean everything up, but decluttering is for your own good.

FOOL'S FABLE

to find everything, it's consolidated all in one place.

Another great way to define something's place is to designate baskets or storage bins for those particular things. This is a great strategy if you've got small children. Have a basket or two in each room where the children play, and just throw all of their toys into the baskets. It's amazing how a basket of toys can look so quaint and yet a floor covered with toys is a nightmare.

Go Digital

Family photos and home movies can take up a lot of space, and in most homes they're susceptible to humidity and even mold, which can quickly destroy them. One way to solve both problems is to convert your photos and movies to CDs or DVDs. Not only can you compress several boxes of photos onto a single disc, but they'll be better protected as well. Just to be safe, make a few copies and store them in safe places, like a safe deposit box.

If you're technologically savvy, you can easily scan your photos and probably figure out how to convert your home movies to DVD format. If you're like we are, you'll probably want to take everything to a digital processing shop and have the experts do it for you. The hardest part of the whole process is bringing yourself to throw away all of your old photos. Even the least nostalgic among us can have a tough time with that. We certainly couldn't blame you if you just couldn't do it, but if you can you will really make a dent in your clutter.

Go Vertical

We have a friend who builds custom cabinetry, and he tells us that the one element of custom cabinets that his clients love the most is that they can determine exactly how much vertical space each shelf will have and can maximize their storage capacity. Therefore, particularly tall items can find a place to be stowed away and small things like spice jars won't take up an entire shelf and leave eight inches of empty air space above them.

Utilizing empty space is probably the most effective way to eliminate clutter throughout your house. Let's take a look at a few different ways to make the most of your unused airspace.

First of all, make sure you've got a stepstool for reaching up to the tops of your closets. Since you'll be storing things there that don't get used frequently, it's not a problem that they won't be so easily accessible. The best way to store things up high is in boxes. That way, you're not stuffing odd-shaped objects up there that will fall or roll off. Measure the height and depth of the space, and find yourself boxes that will fit in there. Then just fill them up and tuck them away.

Another underutilized space is the closet floor, particularly underneath clothing or jackets. You can get yourself drawer units that fit down there, or use small cubby-type cabinets for storing bulky sweaters or anything else that will fit.

As we said earlier, kitchen cabinets can be particularly inefficient. You might have two or three shelves per cabinet, and some shelves might hold coffee mugs or other small items, leaving lots of unused space below the next shelf. One way to solve this problem, and instantly increase your kitchen storage, is to add a shelf. It can actually be a pretty simple process:

1. Check the inside walls of your cabinet. If you see two columns of shallow holes running up each side, then proceed to the next step. If, on the other hand, you have older-style cabinets that

don't use pins to support the shelves, it's still worth looking into shelf organizers that can help maximize the storage space. Visit your local hardware store for ideas.

2. Clear off one of the shelves and lift it out of the cabinet. Remove one of the four pins that supported the shelf.

3. Take the shelf and the pin to a hardware store, which should sell both the shelf stock and the pins. You can either have them cut the stock to the correct width, or do it yourself. When you're purchasing extra pins, just be sure to get the right size (there are two standard sizes, $\frac{1}{4}$ inch and 5 mm).

4. When you get home, remove the remaining original pins and replace them at a more efficient height and reinstall the shelf. Then place the pins for the new shelf and install it.

BRIGHTENING

One misconception about lighting that gets people into trouble is that they believe more light is always better. In fact, too much light, specifically too much artificial light, can be as big a problem as too little light. You don't want to create a hard, antiseptic atmosphere. Nobody walks into a hospital ward and thinks, "Gee, this is quite cozy; I think I'd really like to live here." So rather than just increasing the wattage throughout your house, you should focus on increasing the amount of natural light and making sure your lighting maximizes your home's appeal.

1. Open up all the blinds and curtains throughout your house. If you have big, heavy drapes, consider removing them altogether. Not only do they block light, but they weigh down the room making it feel much smaller. Check to make sure trees and bushes are trimmed to let in as much natural light as possible.

2. Repaint the interior walls in a light, neutral color. White is too harsh and contributes to the hospital feel.

3. Use indirect lighting (such as wall sconces that shine upward or track lighting pointed up or into corners) to add soft light and draw the eyes upward, increasing the sense of space in the room.

4. Minimize the use of fluorescent bulbs, and make sure to use frosted and other soft-light bulbs.

5. Accentuate the positive by adequately lighting your home's best features. If a bedroom has high ceilings, make sure the room fills with light to emphasize the volume of the space. Use undercabinet lights in the kitchen to show off all the counter space.

6. Look at someone else in every room of your house. Do they look good? If they look pasty and pale, you've got too much light. If you see sharp shadows, your light is probably too directed and needs to be diffused. If they look kind of green, you may have too many fluorescent lights. As you walk around the room or between rooms, notice transitions into the shadows and try to lighten up dark spots.

The Feng Shui Lady

You know two California girls couldn't get through a chapter on staging your house without including some discussion of feng shui. Now, before you start rolling your eyes and jumping ahead in the book, let us assure you that we won't get all preachy and we won't suggest that you burn incense or memorize any ritual chants to help ensure a successful sale. But we do think there's something interesting about feng shui, and it is worth exploring a bit as you work to sell your house. At the very least it offers an intriguing philosophy regarding how we exist within our homes. Beyond that, who's to say there's no benefit to designing your home for optimal energy flow and spiritual well-being? We've always been curious about exactly what feng shui is, and if we could possibly use it to help our clients. To get the answers, we interviewed Kirsten Lagatree, author of *Feng Shui: Arranging Your Home to Change Your Life.*

D&S: As we're sure you've noticed, the only experience many people have with feng shui is when it's the punch line of a joke. Or, if someone does actually know something about it, it's usually just enough to know when a place has bad feng shui. Hopefully we can bridge the huge gap in understanding that exists out there. Let's start at the beginning: what is feng shui and why is it important?

Kirsten: Feng shui literally translates as "wind water." It is an ancient Chinese philosophy based on achieving harmony with nature. Basically, feng shui is a set of guidelines for how to live optimally within the natural world. You can achieve this ideal state, according to feng shui, primarily in two ways. First, you need to harness the power of the energy that is all around us (known as chi, pronounced "chee"), which is thought to carry the life force. Second, you want to achieve a balance between the natural opposites of yin and yang, which you see all around you in the forms of male and female, hard and soft, hot and cold, and so on. What I find so fascinating about feng shui is that it provides very specific instructions for how to live. In fact, entire cities in ancient China were built to conform to these principles.

D&S: Can you give us an example of these principles?

Kirsten: Sure, here's one that applies directly to home sellers: According to feng shui, the direction south governs fame and fortune, and the color red is lucky and associated with heat, life, and happiness. So, if you want to make sure that your house is a "hot property," place something red on a south-facing wall.

D&S: Seriously? That seems a little too weird even for us.

Kirsten: I get that reaction from a lot of people, and I totally understand where they're coming from. This type of philosophy is totally foreign to most Westerners, although I've recently heard about Americans burying statues of St. Joseph to bring them luck when selling their homes. Nonetheless, I wouldn't expect your clients to embrace the more esoteric elements of feng shui right away.

Most feng shui novices respond better to its more practical guidelines. And you may be interested to know that feng shui has its roots in that exact same practicality. For example, the importance of the direction south in feng shui dates back thousands of years to when Chinese farmers first began developing the philosophy. They discovered that buildings facing north bore the brunt of dust storms that blew down from Mongolia, and that south-facing buildings not only were protected from the storms but also were better warmed by the sun.

D&S: Couldn't you then argue that the direction south doesn't hold any universal spiritual significance but just happened to be important to those Chinese farmers?

Kirsten: Absolutely, and that's why I wouldn't expect sellers to feel any great urge to follow the particular edicts of feng shui. The value of the philosophy for skeptical sellers comes from the general idea of finding harmony with nature and opening up spaces. If you abide by the general principles of feng shui, regardless of whether or not you believe there's any spiritual consequence to doing so, you'll undoubtedly find that your home is more peaceful, more comfortable, and more appealing to prospective buyers.

D&S: That's exactly what we find so compelling about feng shui. Even though we don't necessarily know if there's any great significance to the direction south (fame and fortune) or the color green (health and harmony) or the number six (long life), the principles of feng shui eventually lead to almost exactly the same place we guide our clients to as they prepare to sell their homes. With that in mind, what are some other elements of feng shui that sellers can easily relate to?

Kirsten: As you both know so well, removing clutter from your house is a great way to increase its appeal to buyers. Within feng shui, you remove clutter to allow chi to flow more freely throughout the house (oversized furniture is a particularly powerful chi blocker). We would all agree that an uncluttered space is more appealing

WORDS FROM THE WISE

than one full of random stuff. Maybe feng shui helps explain *why* we feel that way.

It's the same with ambience. We almost universally agree when a home has a pleasant, welcoming ambience, but it's hard to pinpoint why that is. It's possible that we have an innate preference for the well-lit, airy, and balanced interior design that feng shui dictates.

You shouldn't allow your trees or shrubs to overgrow up against your house. You would tell sellers that it blocks natural light; feng shui says that there's an imbalance, with the yin of the trees imposing on the yang of the house, and that's a bad thing. Either way, you need to cut the trees and shrubs back.

That balance should carry over throughout. For example, you want to balance a concrete patio with greenery, and you want to balance a stainless-steel kitchen with natural-wood cabinets.

I know you both believe very strongly that the front porch or entranceway is one of the most important elements of a house. Feng shui says that you want your entranceway to be perfect to make guests feel welcome and respected.

D&S: We've actually had clients look at us as we approached the front door and ask, "Weren't they expecting us?" That's always a bad sign. Hopefully some of our readers will want to explore feng shui more seriously, and even incorporate some elements within their house when they sell. What are some traditional feng shui things they can do?

Kirsten: I've got plenty of examples, and I've found that even people who try these things for the first time receive some benefit from them. Maybe there's some truth to the philosophy, or maybe it just makes them feel more comfortable and happier in their home and buyers pick up on that. Either way, I truly believe that good feng shui is good selling.

Feng shui homes will often have mirrors or reflective tiles behind the stove. This is done for two reasons. First, the cooks can see what's going on behind them so they won't be surprised. Second, the mirror image symbolically doubles the food, creating a sense of abundance. You'll also often find mirrors in the dining room, which not only doubles the food but also doubles the number of guests.

Also in the kitchen, you don't want to place the stove next to the sink, since the water would symbolically extinguish the flame of the stove. And you don't want anything red in the kitchen, which would overheat the room.

You also don't want red in your bedroom, which would attract too many spirits and disturb your sleep. The foot of the bed should not be facing directly toward the door, since that's where the bed of a dying person is placed so that the body can easily be removed from the room after they're gone. If you have no choice but to face your bed that way, place a low chest at the foot of the bed to break the line.

Bathrooms should not be located near the kitchen, for obvious reasons. Actually, according to feng shui, bathrooms shouldn't even be inside the house. If you're not particularly interested in moving the bathroom, a simple solution is to hang a mirror outside the bathroom door to deflect the negative energy. Finally, for all you ladies out there who can't get your men to put the toilet seat down, explain to them that according to feng shui they're letting good fortune go down the toilet.

WORDS FROM THE WISE

SETTING THE STAGE

Now that we've given you an introduction to the basic techniques of staging, let's go through your house room by room and set the stage in each one so that buyers will enjoy the total experience of the wonderful life they might have in your house.

Staging the Kitchen

A recent study by Equation Research asked homeowners to think about how they decorate their homes and which rooms mattered most to them. Fifty-three percent of homeowners were most concerned about the decor in their living rooms, with kitchens a distant second at under 20 percent. But, when they were asked which rooms mattered most to them when they were *buying* their homes, over 50 percent said the kitchen mattered most. This means there's a disconnect between what home*owners* think is important and what home *buyers* want in a home, and it explains why many sellers don't pay enough attention to staging their kitchens. Until now! Let's get in the kitchen and start staging.

1. Your kitchen countertop should be completely empty, with two exceptions: (1.) You are allowed one appliance (but make sure it's in perfect condition) and (2) there may be one bowl of *fresh* fruit, including a lemon.

2. Remove everything from in and around the sink. All soap, sponges, dish racks, and so on should be stored out of sight.

3. Clean and organize the cabinet under the sink. For some reason men always look under there. It's probably like looking under the hood of a car. They may not even know what they're looking for, but it just seems manly to look.

4. In case you didn't believe us the first time we said it, you really should clean your kitchen floor with a sponge rather than a mop. It really benefits from the extra attention.

5. If you have a ceiling fan in your kitchen, make sure the blades are clean. Kitchen ceiling fans often look like they've got something resembling Spanish moss hanging from them.

6. Clean all of the cabinet doors, especially those closer to the stove, which are probably coated with grease. Any window treatments are also probably greasy and should be removed or replaced.

7. If you have a garden window, clear it of everything except a few plants. Keep your plants looking fresh or buy new ones. When you do buy new plants, keep the plants in their plastic containers, drop them into nice ceramic pots, and cover them with moss or stones. Then, if that plant withers, be sure to replace it with a new one.

8. Make sure the trash can is out of sight, even if it's covered. Plan on emptying the trash much more frequently than usual.

9. Clean the stove inside and out, and make sure the dishwasher is empty (or at least that the dishes in it are clean).

10. If you can, move the pet's food and water bowls out of the kitchen.

11. If there's any kind of throw rug or mat in the kitchen, you should probably get rid of it. More than likely it's not as clean as it should be, and it makes the kitchen look smaller.

12. Prospective buyers usually don't open the refrigerator unless it's built in and obviously will be sold with the house. Either way, it's worthwhile to clean out the fridge and put a new box of baking soda in there. But it's a higher priority if your fridge is built-in.

13. If you have a kitchen table, make sure it's completely clear of papers, homework, and anything else that might accumulate on it. You can put a nice vase of fresh flowers there, or just leave it empty. There's some debate as to whether you should set the table or not.

Donna: There's a bit of a generation gap when it comes to setting the table for a showing. I think it looks nice and inviting . . .

Shannon: While I think it's just cheesy. We have the same disagreement about whether you should put a bottle of champagne and champagne flutes by a hot tub. I think it looks too much like the set of *Three's Company.*

Donna: I guess it depends on the rest of the decor in your house. If your house is more traditional, place settings can look classy, but if you've got a simple, contemporary look going, they would seem out of place. I still think the champagne is a nice touch.

Steel Appeal

Stainless-steel appliances have been all the rage for years, and their appeal seems to be holding steady. If you have stainless-steel appliances, you've probably come to realize that while they may look great at first, it's not easy to keep them that way. Sure, they don't stain exactly, but they scratch quite easily and will pick up more fingerprints than an entire season of *CSI*. On the positive side, it's possible to get them looking almost new again, if you use the right product. For us, the right product for renewing stainless steel is Bar Keepers Friend. We love this stuff, and use it on just about every type of surface. For stainless steel, though, it works better than anything else we've tried. It softens scratches and removes fingerprints completely. If you can't find it in stores, you can purchase it directly from the Web site: www.barkeepersfriend.com.

INSIDER SECRET

Staging the Bathroom

We're not sure exactly why it is, but buyers always seem to remember the quality of the bathrooms. Given this high regard, and how messy they can get with regular use, bathrooms require vigilant attention while your home is on the market. Here's just a sample of tasks you need to do to create and maintain a well-staged bathroom.

1. If you didn't buy the bath mat last week, get a new one. Then, the day before any showings, throw the bath mat (and any hand towels) in the dryer with a scented dryer sheet.

2. If the toilet seat shows any imperfections, replace it, too. Make sure the lid is down for any showings.

3. We definitely prefer either white or off-white towels in the bathroom, and keep them to a minimum. You can get a great price on new towels (and other housewares) at Marshalls, T.J.Maxx, or Ross.

4. Make sure the bathroom trash can is completely empty for every showing.

5. Get everything out of the shower except one bottle of shampoo, one bottle of conditioner, and soap.

6. Make sure there are no stray hairs anywhere in the bathroom. It's amazing how many people get totally grossed out by hair. We

have hair allover our bodies, but if one gets stuck on the shower wall we end up cupping water in our hands and trying to splash it down the drain rather than actually touching it.

7. Replace the shower curtain and the curtain rings. Get a fabric curtain rather than a plastic one, and avoid any patterns on the curtain.

8. Bathrooms don't need to be particularly bright, but you need good light by the mirrors. People will look at themselves, so the mirrors should also be spotless. Keep a clean cloth in the bathroom to wipe down the mirrors, faucets, and sinks every day that the house will be shown.

9. If you have carpeting in your bathroom that's not brand new or in perfect condition, you should probably replace it. Any imperfections will cause buyers to wonder what lies beneath. And remember, since bathrooms are a primary source of bad smells, carpeting can easily add to the mix. In fact, even if you don't have carpeting in the bathroom be sure to use an air freshener, clear out the drains, clean the toilet, and empty the trash can.

10. Clear off the countertop completely. You may leave soap there, but replace bar soap with liquid hand soap. Other than that, only a neatly folded hand towel and fresh flowers are allowed.

Staging the Bedrooms

They say that the kitchen is the new living room, with families spending much of their time together there, either cooking, eating, doing homework, or even watching TV. Believe it or not, we're also spending much more "together time" in the bedrooms. Teenagers have always created a miniuniverse in their bedrooms, but now it seems that adults are following their example. With wireless Internet and satellite multimedia systems, bedrooms are becoming public spaces within the house. Keep this in mind as you stage the bedroom, leaving it open, airy, and inviting, and take into consideration the following tips.

1. If you've seen *The Sopranos,* you want your bedroom to be the exact opposite of Tony and Carmela's bedroom.

2. Side tables should be completely clear, except for a lamp and possibly a flower.

3. Be sure the bed is perfectly made and all fluffed up (see "Beds Gone Wild!" below).

4. Buyers will look in your closets, so put your clothes on wooden hangers and face them all the same way, turn the light on if you have one, and arrange your shoes neatly.

5. Make sure your clothes hamper is in a closet and that it has a lid. Actually, it's more important for your hamper to have a lid than for your trash cans to have one.

Beds Gone Wild!

You "more experienced" ladies will probably remember the good ol' days when there were dozens of different types of panty hose to choose from. It was overwhelming. These days, you'll probably feel the same way as you shop for bedding. If you've stayed in any trendy hotels lately, you've probably noticed that the bed had more buildup than Austin Powers's teeth. It's like peeling back the layers of an onion to find the sheet that you're actually supposed to sleep on. The effect is extremely luxurious, with beds becoming architectural creations, all cozy and poofy with different types of pillows and comforters looking like risen bread dough on steroids.

This is yet another example of a staging strategy that's effective, yet completely impractical in real life. Buyers see a luxuriously adorned bed and they imagine themselves living full time at a Ritz-Carlton hotel. We know it sounds crazy, but who are we to dismiss their fantasy, particularly if it means they're willing to sweeten their offer.

So, go out to Bed Bath & Beyond, look at the most appealing beds they have on display, and try to emulate that at home. It's probably been a long time since you bought new bedding anyway. Why not buy the new bedding before you leave, use it to improve your staging (it might even pay for itself by increasing your sale price a bit), and then take it all with you when you leave?

6. Downplay the decor in a nursery or child's room so prospective buyers can visualize the room as something else, most likely a guest room or an office. For example, remove the glow-in-the-dark constellations that are stuck to the ceiling and repaint the room a neutral color (be sure to use a primer/sealer over crayon or other markers). If you have plain linens, use them instead of the *Finding Nemo* sheets. Also, it's very important to declutter a child's room, since it's probably one of the busiest rooms in the house. Remove anything that won't send your child into a hysterical tantrum, and remove any unnecessary furniture or decor.

Staging the Living Room

The living room is an important space to focus on because it's usually the first room that buyers see after they enter the house. It's also important because living rooms often include many personal touches. This is the room where sellers get most offended when we suggest changes, since they often see the living room as more a reflection of their tastes than the other rooms in the house. So, let's all take a deep breath, remember that your house is just a commodity, and see what we can do.

1. Either move all of the furniture into the middle of the living room, or remove it altogether. Get rid of any extraneous

pieces—unattached bookshelves, for example—and then put
back everything that's left.

2. If possible, arrange your furniture so that the traffic lines move
diagonally across the room, which will make the room feel
larger. Enter the room through each entryway and make sure
nothing blocks your path.

3. Oversized furniture is probably the most common staging mistake we see. It can make a room look small and dominate the
decor above everything else. Try to remove one piece (the love
seat or a recliner) to open up the room.

4. There really shouldn't be any brightly colored childern's plastic
furniture in the living room. This is an adults-only space.

5. Remove all personal photos, particularly wedding pictures.

6. Make sure the floor is spotless. Buyers want to imagine their
kids playing down there.

7. If your television is too big for the room, you should remove it
while the house is on the market. And unless you have a dedicated screening room, any big-screen TV is probably too big
for the room it's in. We've had clients who put giant-screen
TVs in front of bay windows and even doors. Move the TV to
the garage or a friend's house (we're sure they'll gladly take it
off your hands for a while). If you must keep the giant TV, just
understand that you will most likely be leaving money on the
table when you sell the house.

8. Be sure that area rugs are clean. If not, either deep clean them
or replace them. Keep the colors light and the patterns minimal. The fewer different colors you have, the larger the room
will appear.

9. If you've got an old chair or couch and can't replace it, buy some new throw pillows from IKEA to dress it up quickly. If the cushions are obviously stained or dingy, you should definitely replace the couch. Remember, if you're going to replace it after you move, you should buy it before you sell and use the new couch to improve your staging (just remember to insure it for replacement value when you move).

Staging the Outdoors

It's official: the outdoors is the new indoors. Even in notoriously awful climates (we feel your pain, really we do), homeowners are devoting more and more attention to what's going on outside of their houses. According to the American Institute of Architects' Home Design Trends survey, interest in outdoor design has increased dramatically. The most recent survey found that 64 percent of the architecture firms believed that there was growing demand for outdoor living spaces among their clients. Regardless of whether you live in sunny Southern California, rainy Seattle, or snowy New England, you want to maximize the positive impact that your outdoor space—however limited it may be—will have on prospective buyers.

Curb Appeal, of Course   Everybody talks about curb appeal, but it's not that easy to define exactly. For us, curb appeal means that when a buyer is driving or walking down your street checking out all the houses on the block, they suddenly see your house and desperately want that to be the one for sale. Then, when they see the house number and realize it is the house for sale, they can't wait to go inside and check it out. As an exercise, approach your house with a buyer's eyes and see if you experience that same sensation. If not, think about exactly why not and get to work. One mistake that many sellers make is that they move their cars out of the garage or the driveway but park them in the street right out front. Remember, it's called *curb* appeal, not double-park appeal. If prospective buyers have to double-park in front of your house, they won't be able to stop and take a leisurely look at your house, and they'll get the sense that parking is more difficult on your street than it actually may be.

Shannon: You know, Mom, there is one benefit to having bad curb appeal, at least while you're living in your house and not selling it.

Donna: Really, what's that?

Shannon: It's a great security system. My house has awful curb appeal, so I know that no self-respecting burglar will ever think there's anything valuable inside.

Donna: Nice rationalization, Shan.

This may seem totally ridiculous, but we both have a pet peeve about metal thresholds under front doors. You may not even know whether yours is metal or wood, but it's one of the first things we notice about a house. A wooden threshold is just a much nicer way to welcome people into your home.

When clients look at us like we're crazy, we tell them that if we have a pet peeve about this, odds are someone else does, too. So, if you're having other carpentry done anyway, replace the threshold. You won't regret it.

TOP-DOLLAR TIP

The Drive-by Viewing

Rather than accompanying their buyers to several open houses every weekend, some agents will just recommend that their clients drive around the neighborhood and see homes they like with FOR SALE signs out front (even we admit to having done this a few times over the years). If your house is lacking in curb appeal, some buyers will take a quick look and just keep on driving. In fact, we've made personal appointments for buyers to view a house, but when they approached the house they decided not to go in and canceled the appointment—just based on the view from the curb!

Declutter   Just as you decluttered in the inside of your house, you also want to clear out the outdoor space as much as possible. The outdoors represents what we like to call subliminal square footage, which means it's not officially included in the square footage of the house, but outdoor space that feels large and inviting can make the whole house seem larger to a prospective buyer.

Connect Inside and Out   Another way to increase your subliminal square footage is to make visual connections between the indoors and the outdoors. The idea is to draw the buyer's eyes outside as they're exploring inside, creating the sensation of a larger space overall. To do this, coordinate your outdoor design with the indoor decor. Use the same colors and patterns, and try to make it feel like the outdoor space is a natural extension of the room inside. It goes without saying that immaculately clean windows are essential (see "How-to Hint: Wash the Windows" on page 183). And, of course, if you've properly staged the outdoors people will want to go there. So make sure that all of the doors open smoothly and that you have new doormats by every door.

Hose It Down   Many sellers neglect to wash the outside of their houses. This is a cheap and easy way to make a quick improvement. Just rent a power washer, connect it to your hose, and go for it. On a warm, sunny day you can actually have a great time power-washing your house. Be careful, though, as a powerful washer can leave marks on your siding. Also, don't try to power-wash your spouse at point-blank range; it can really sting.

Focus on the Front Porch   We'll bet you never realized that your front porch is among the most important spaces in your house. Imagine this

Subliminal Square Footage

Subliminal square footage is the space that is not included in the calculation of your home's square footage but that nonetheless can be used to make your home *feel* larger.

BUZZWORD

scenario: The buyers and their agent arrive for a scheduled viewing. The buyers are very eager to get inside, visualizing their dream home just behind that front door. It takes a few minutes for the agent to open the lockbox, remove the key, and open the door. During that time, the buyers carefully examine every square inch of the front porch, looking up, down, and sideways to determine if this house will live up to their expectations. To make sure they are not disappointed, take the following steps.

1. Make sure the porch is spotless. That means cleaning out any spider webs (and getting all the dead bugs out of the light fixture), repainting the door, replacing the doormat, and adding some potted plants.

2. Make sure the doorbell works (don't just tape over the button). For a quick fix, install a wireless doorbell.

3. Consider adding a brass kick plate on the door if it works with your decor.

4. Make sure the key works smoothly and the door opens easily (and silently). You don't want the buyer's agent to struggle with the front door or have it open with a spooky creak. Use silicone spray on the lock and hinges. If the doorknob is also dull, tarnished, and scratched, just replace it altogether.

5. Because a security door out front indicates an unsafe neighborhood, if it is no longer necessary, take it off. If every house has one, and it's necessary for your safety, it's not worth the risk to remove it.

Plant Power   If you're like us and can kill any plant in just days with the touch of your hand, properly staging all of the outdoor greenery can be quite a challenge. With all of the other craziness involved in selling your house, it's probably worthwhile to hire a landscaper or gardener to get everything looking healthy and lush and to make sure your landscaping doesn't obscure the best possible view of the house or block too much light from the inside. Be sure to tell your gardener exactly when the house will be on the market, so that he or she can prune and fertilize accordingly. For example, it might be healthiest for certain trees to be cut way back every few years, but you don't want the centerpiece of your yard looking like Charlie Brown's puny little Christmas tree. Also, you don't want to cut back plants that provide a sense of privacy, which is a desirable feature in a yard.

On the other hand, you should be rather aggressive when it comes to removing limbs hanging over your house or your neighbor's property. You can be sure that buyers will notice them and add it to their ever-growing list of things they'll have to do if they buy your house. (If you're really unlucky, the threatening limb will decide that the morning of your first open house is the ideal time to take the plunge and crash through the kitchen ceiling.)

Curve Appeal

Try to soften any sharp angles or long straight pathways by adding round planters in corners or along the path. This strategy could also work indoors, if you have an empty corner. By the way, this strategy is good feng shui, since sharp angles can deflect chi while curves help smooth its path.

Wet and Wild   Water features such as pools, spas, and fountains can add value to your home, but they also present risks. Pools and spas may be luxury items to some buyers but expensive inconveniences to others. Make sure your pool or spa is perfectly clean and in excellent working order (for example, noisy pumps should be repaired or replaced). These amenities also present serious safety concerns for buyers, particularly those with young children. Make sure all safety measures, such as a fence around the pool and lock on the spa lid, are properly installed and functional.

Fountains can create a wonderful ambience and can help block traffic and other street noise. But there are risks here, too. We find that a surprising number of fountains don't work, and the homeowners have forgotten about them. If you can't repair a broken fountain, then remove it. Also, be sure to keep the algae under control, and treat the water regularly if you have fish, turtles, or other aquatic critters.

Outdoor Accessories   You want to leave just enough furniture and other items to give buyers a sense of how they can use the outdoor space. Make sure the furniture matches and is all clean or new. At the least you should plan on replacing any cushions on the chairs or chaise lounges.

For some reason, we find that many people who collect stuff feel compelled to share their collections with the world by displaying them outside. There's one house that we frequently drive by which displays what must be the Western Hemisphere's largest collection of rusty teakettles. Suffice it to say that you need to remove any outdoor collections just as you did with indoor ones.

How-to Hint: Wash the Windows

As we mentioned above, there are strategies you can employ to draw buyers' attention outside. For those strategies to be successful, you have to make sure buyers can actually see the outside. Washing your windows is one of the single best improvements you can make to your house before selling. You'll be amazed at how much brighter and more appealing your home will be afterward. It's not particularly expensive to hire someone, but it's amazingly cheap to do yourself. In fact, an analysis at Home Gain.com found that washing the windows yourself can yield almost 800 percent return on investment. And, believe it or not, washing windows isn't that hard. With the proper equipment, and by following these simple steps, you might even have a little fun.

1. *Forget about washing windows with Windex and paper towels. It makes the task laborious and you'll almost always end up with streaks or lint on the glass. Go to Lowe's or Home Depot and get yourself a squeegee, a scrubber sponge with a handle, and white terry-cloth hand towels. You can probably find a kit that includes everything you'll need.*

2. *Remove any screens or storm windows. Screens can be washed with soapy water and allowed to air-dry. Storm windows can be cleaned with the same technique that you'll use for the windows themselves.*

3. *To make your window-washing solution, add ½ cup ammonia and ½ cup vinegar to one gallon of warm water.*

4. *Soak the scrubber sponge in the cleaning solution and apply to the window. With the terry-cloth towel, wipe a dry line across the top of the windowpane. Now make vertical swipes with the squeegee to clean the window. Use the towel again to remove any lines.*

Cleaning Windows

1. Do not clean windows on very hot days or in direct sunlight. They'll dry too quickly and leave streaks.

2. If you clean the inside of your windows with the technique above (moving the squeegee vertically), on the outside of the windows wipe the squeegee across horizontally. That way, if there are streaks, you'll know which side of the window they're on.

3. To clean windowsills, first vacuum out any dirt and dust, and then wipe the sill with a damp cloth.

4. To keep windows from sticking, rub a thin film of petroleum jelly on the inside of the window trim.

INSIDER SECRET

Whole-House Staging Suggestions

Many staging suggestions work in more than one room of your house. Here are a few tips to keep in mind regardless of where you are.

Baby-Proofing   If you have small children and your house is baby-proofed, do the best you can to minimize its impact without compromising the safety of your child. Pay close attention to any locks that will be difficult to unlatch and make sure every room of the house is accessible.

Stage for the Seasons   Make sure you don't have Christmas decorations up in March or summer accessories around the house in November.

Staging Your Pets   Be honest with yourself—are your pets perfectly well-behaved around strangers? If not, board them during showings. One time while showing a house, Donna was pinned in the garage by a vicious Doberman. It might have been funny if she hadn't been so terrified. Eventually, she snuck over to the fridge, grabbed a hot dog, and tossed it back into the garage. The dog sprinted in after it and she locked him inside for the duration of the showing.

Also, you should probably remove any potentially creepy pets from the house. Dogs and cats are fine, but snakes, spiders, and lizards have to go.

Climate Control   Make sure your house is comfortably cool in the summer and warm in the winter. That way, buyers will want to linger inside as long as possible. If you've got an old thermostat, replace it with a new programmable one so you can set the temperature exactly where you want it for showings.

Open-House Checklist

Assuming you've already taken care of the more complicated preparations and staging, here is a checklist of basic things you should do before leaving your house *every time* it is going to be shown.

- ✓ Grind half a lemon in the garbage disposal.
- ✓ Make sure all of the toilet lids (not just the seats) are down.
- ✓ Empty every trash can.
- ✓ Open windows and curtains (outdoor noise and weather permitting).
- ✓ Wipe down all the sinks, faucets, and mirrors.
- ✓ Empty the dishwasher.
- ✓ Make sure that your fresh flowers actually look fresh. Remove any wilted or dead flowers.

continued

✓ Turn on the lights in any dark rooms or hallways.

✓ Turn on classical music.

✓ Close the shower curtain.

✓ Fluff up the pillows and bedspread.

✓ If you have cats, clean out the litter box.

✓ Sweep off the front porch.

✓ Shut all the closet doors.

✓ Be sure that everything is off the floor that shouldn't be there (clothes, toys, papers, vacuum, ironing board, etc.).

✓ Spray lightly scented air freshener in the kitchen and bathrooms.

✓ Put away any mail or newspapers.

6

Close the Deal

MOST SELLERS ASSUME that their agent's primary role is to list their house on the Multiple Listing Service and to host prospective buyers and agents at open houses. In fact, that's the easiest part of the job. The most important and complicated parts of our job take place once the house has been shown and interested buyers begin submitting offers. That's when it gets interesting (and possibly quite messy as well).

The more you understand about what's going on at this stage, regardless of how involved you have been up to that point, the more efficiently you can work with your agent and the more smoothly the transaction is likely to go.

ACCEPTING AN OFFER

You've worked really hard to this point, finding the right agent and preparing your house for the market. Up until now you've had reasonable control over the process. Now it's time to see what the market will bear, but there's still plenty for you to do. In fact, being active and involved at this point is crucial to accomplishing your goals.

Be Prepared

The first step to retaining control over the process of accepting an offer is to set well-informed and realistic expectations. Keep a close eye on the current market and talk to your agent about where he or she thinks the market is headed and how strong or weak it is. Review your goals once again and remind yourself what is most important to you. Also, what are your alternatives if things don't go according to plan? Can you take the house off the market? Could you rent it out? Knowing all of these things in advance will prevent you from being distracted by whatever situation may arise during the process. Finally, you want to figure out your bottom line.

Keep Your Bottom Line in Mind

Your bottom line is the absolute lowest price you could conceivably accept and still be better off than if you chose one of your alternative plans. This is *not* a price that you should expect to ever accept but just a "floor" to keep in mind when entertaining offers. We're usually very confident that the listing price we've selected is an accurate reflection of the value of a house. But when sellers know their lowest acceptable price it helps them see the big picture and not focus exclusively on meeting or beating their asking price.

Once you know your bottom line, you'll have an easy way to determine whether an offer is even in your ballpark, which can help you deal with the offer more objectively. Often sellers get offended when they receive offers even just a few thousand dollars below their asking price. But with a bottom line in mind, you'll immediately know if an offer is reasonable and whether you can deal with it constructively.

You'll probably need to work with your agent to collect the information you need to calculate your bottom line, but we actually don't recommend that you share your final figure with your agent. It's not likely, but it is possible that your agent could subconsciously communicate this information to the buyer, which would jeopardize your negotiation.

We've based our method for calculating your lowest acceptable price on a book called *The Heart and Mind of the Negotiator* by Leigh Thompson. Here's how it works:

Working with your agent, determine the probability that you'll sell your house for the asking price within the average days on the market for comparable local properties. It's impossible to know the exact probability, but it's more important to be realistic than to be perfect. In this case, let's use as an example the probability of a house listed for $400,000 selling in one month. Assuming you priced your house correctly and prepared it well, the probability of getting close to or right at your asking price should be pretty high, but of course it depends on your local market. In an average market we would guess that any house we list for sale has a 70 percent chance of selling for listing price within the local average market time.

If there's an 70 percent chance that the house will sell for the asking price in one month, then there's a 30 percent chance that something else will happen. The next step is to determine the likelihood of the other possible outcomes. For example, you might believe that if you lower the price to $360,000, there will be a 90 percent chance of selling at that price. That leaves a 10 percent chance of not selling even at that lower price. In this case, you might decide to rent out the house for two years with a net rental income of $30,000 for that period.

To simplify our calculation, we're only going to explore one possible alternative outcome: lowering your asking price to guarantee a sale (that is, to have a 100 percent probability of it selling within a certain amount of time). In our example, we believe that lowering the asking price to $350,000 will guarantee that the house will sell in two months. Remember, these are just educated guesses, based on the current market and the condition of the house.

To calculate your bottom line, multiply the probability of the event occurring by the amount of money you're likely to receive from that event, and then add the results together. Our sample transaction is illustrated in the chart "Bottom-Line Worksheet" opposite, so let's walk through it. Starting from the left side of the chart, you can see that when your house goes on the market, there's a 70 percent chance of selling for the listing price of $400,000 within the average local listing time. You then multiply those two numbers together (400,000 × .70) to get $280,000.

Now let's walk through the other scenario. There's a 30 percent chance that your house doesn't sell for the listing price.

If you lower the asking price to $350,000, we believe the house will definitely sell within two months. The calculation for that scenario is to multiply the 30 percent chance of not getting your asking price by the 100 percent chance of selling at a lower price, multiplied by the reduced price ($350,000).

When you add these numbers together, you find that your gross bottom line is $385,000. But that figure doesn't take into account the costs you bear of keeping your house on the market for that time. You need to add up your mortgage, insurance, taxes, and other maintenance costs for the entire three months (the initial one month listing at the original price and then the possible two additional months at the lower price) and subtract that amount to get your net bottom line. In this case, the carrying costs are $10,000 for the three months, so the actual bottom line for this seller is $375,000.

As we said before, you shouldn't assume that you'd have to accept that amount. Just keep in mind that any offer above that amount is in the ballpark and would be a better option than the alternatives, so you should seriously consider it. Use the "Bottom-Line Worksheet" below to help determine your bottom line.

We mentioned earlier that it can get complicated if the likely sale price for your house is less than you owe on the mortgage (a "short sell"). In fact, even if your bottom line is less than you owe, you should have a serious discussion with your agent about your best course of action.

Bottom-Line Worksheet

What is the listing price for your house? $ _____

How likely is it to sell at that price?   (A) _____ %

Multiply those two numbers together: (1) _____

What's your average local market time?   _____ weeks

What are your total carrying costs for that time?   (X) _____ weeks

Subtract the value of (A) from 100%:   (B) _____ %

To what would you have to lower your price
to guarantee it selling? $ _____

Multiply that amount x (B):   (2) _____

How long would that take?   _____ months

What are your total carrying costs for that time?   (Y) _____

Add the values of (1) and (2) $ _____

Subtract the sum of (X) and (Y) $ _____

       BOTTOM LINE $ _____

If more time goes by than you estimated, subtract your additional carrying costs and other expenses to recalculate your bottom line. This does not mean that you should lower your asking price, but just remember that time costs you money and your bottom line will get lower over time.

The bottom line figure that we just calculated is really just a starting point, since it doesn't take many other factors into consideration. To get a more complete picture, you may want to quantify some of the other goals that you set in Step 1. For example, if you need to close quickly you should figure out what that's worth to you. Suppose you want to close as soon as possible, and you determine that a quick closing is worth $5,000. If you're comparing two offers, one that has a short closing and one that has a longer closing, your bottom line will be $5,000 *lower* for the shorter closing. Simply put, the more valuable an offer is on things other than price, the more flexible you can be on price.

Stay in Control

When you receive an offer (or offers, if you are fortunate enough), it's important to remember that *you* start off with the upper hand in any negotiations.

The listing price, which you and your agent originally set, "anchors" the negotiation and is the most salient factor when buyers think about what to offer for the house. While they do look at comparable homes and consider other factors, buyers are powerfully influenced by the asking price when determining your home's value.

You know what your bottom line is, and you've carefully figured your goals, so you have clear boundaries and expectations for the negotiation.

It's relatively easy for buyers to increase their offers. Since they will pay down their loan over many years, adding even several thousand dollars to their offer will result in only a slight increase in their monthly payment. In your case, on the other hand, lowering the asking price takes that money right out of your pocket. Every dollar you lower your asking price is a dollar you won't get at the closing. We're not suggesting that you get greedy and become obsessed with your sale price, but you do need to understand that there is a difference between how you and the buyer will approach the negotiation.

As we move forward through the negotiation process, we'll make sure that you retain as much control as possible.

Stay Open (Minded) for Business

Remember when we talked about distancing yourself emotionally from your house? You have to do the same thing when receiving offers. You should neither feel insulted by very low offers nor should you get overly excited about high ones.

Dealing with low-ball offers (roughly 15–20 percent below the asking price) reminds us of snooty fashion boutique salespeople who look down their noses at people who just browse around the store. The fact is, you never know who the buyer might be, and it just makes good business sense to treat every potential customer with respect. So always keep the lines of communication open. An interested buyer may be inexperienced and might be forcing their agent to submit the offer, which he or she is obligated to submit. A strong counteroffer or simply a written memo would communicate to the buyer that his offer was unreasonable and he needs to increase it substantially.

Be sure that you encourage the buyer to rethink his offer but still maintain the powerful anchor of the listing price. Your communication should invite him to make a better offer (or to improve his stance on other contingencies, like shortening the loan or inspection contingency periods).

Of course, there are some offers that just do not require a

response. Assuming that you and your agent have priced your home at current market value, offers more than 20 percent below the asking price are probably bottom feeders looking for a steal. Offers with outrageous contingencies can show that the buyer isn't serious. For example, we recently received an offer and learned that the buyer wanted a 30-day inspection contingency (an acceptable inspection contingency would be 10–14 days, which gives the buyer plenty of time to get an inspector in there but doesn't delay the process too long). In some cases, though, it's is perfectly acceptable to reject an offer that seems to be more trouble than it's worth. As always, your agent should offer guidance throughout this part of the process.

An Offer You Can't Refuse

Now, let's get to the more realistic scenario of entertaining reasonable offers. A reasonable offer is one that when all of the factors are taken into account, not just the price, is above your bottom line. That means you've considered the contingencies, assigned values to them, and adjusted your bottom line for that offer accordingly.

Oddly enough, receiving a reasonable offer can get sellers into trouble. They start imagining more and higher offers rolling in and they lose sight of their goals. We've seen many sellers reject that first offer, assuming that something better will come along. If the second offer doesn't immediately materialize, they start regretting the decision. Then, when another offer does arrive, it is often accepted hastily despite its shortcomings.

Based on our experience, the first offer you receive above your bottom line will probably be the best overall offer, so you should consider it very seriously. We prefer to make a single counteroffer to any reasonable offer. The problem with going back and forth many times is that as negotiations linger on you could begin to develop an adversarial relationship with the buyer.

Remember, accepting an offer is just the beginning. Once the sales agreement is signed there still could be a lot of negotiation. Don't push for too much too soon, because more than likely you'll eventually have to give something back before the sale is final. For instance, pressuring the buyer to remove contingencies from their offer may embolden them down the road when they're deciding how many repairs to request. Your goal at this point is to accept the best offer, not to make it a perfect offer before you accept it.

We believe that both the buyer and the seller need to come out of this process feeling good about the outcome. For us, that is a successful negotiation.

Consider the Source

We mentioned in Step 2 that there are potential conflicts of interest with real estate agents (see question 8 in "Top Ten Questions to Ask Prospective Agents"). Hopefully your agent disavowed the "double pop," and her agency doesn't offer incentives to keep deals in-house.

If you didn't address this possibility ahead of time, be very wary if your agent brings the buyer to the table. Even if the offer looks great it's extremely risky to have one person representing both sides. If this happens, you should ask your agent to refer the buyer to another agent. And make sure the new agent is from a different office than your agent.

Some agencies offer incentives to agents who keep listings in-house (and out of the MLS), and this also works against your best interests. If you find out that a buyer is represented by someone from your agent's office, you should make sure no such incentives exist. If they do, be sure to review that buyer's offer very closely.

You're not likely to encounter these types of issues (particularly if you're working with an experienced, professional agent), but they're worth knowing about just in case.

NO-BRAINER

Which Offer Is Best?

If you're lucky enough to receive multiple offers, you're faced with the welcome challenge of determining which offer is the best for you. We like to let the interested parties know that multiple offers have been made and ask them to resubmit their final and best offer. Your agent may take a different approach, such as going back to each buyer separately with a counteroffer, but we find that this often drags out the process too long. Discuss this strategy ahead of time with your agent.

When you have all of the offers in hand, it's time to compare them. The most obvious point of comparison is price, but as we discussed when we helped you set your goals, price isn't everything. And just because someone makes a high-priced offer doesn't necessarily mean they're the best buyer for you. To sort through the offers you receive and decide which one truly is the best, compare them side by side and look at all of the important factors of each one.

Sit down with your agent and fill out the chart opposite, looking at how the details of each offer compare. Going row by row, circle the one that most closely matches your goals. For example, start off by circling the highest price (or, if two or more offers are within just a few thousand dollars, circle all of them). Then circle the one with the highest down payment and the best closing date, and indicate whether or not each offer is contingent on the buyer selling their current house. Get a sense of all the other contingencies and rank the offers from most appealing to least with regard to those contingencies (see "The Sales Agreement" on page 201 for a more detailed explanation of contingencies). It might also be useful to ask your agent to give his or her opinion by rank ordering the offers from best to worst.

Then you can look at the chart to see if one offer stands out from the rest. If you find that multiple offers are pretty much the same, you can now confidently opt for the one with the highest price.

Offer 1	Offer 2	Offer 3	
			Price
			Down payment
			Closing date
Yes/No	Yes/No	Yes/No	Buyer's sale of current home
			Contingencies
			Agent's ranking
			Other thoughts

Backup Offers

If you receive more than one reasonable offer you may want to designate a backup offer, which you could accept if the best offer falls through. This is usually an informal agreement with a secondary buyer, whose offer you'll consider before putting the house back on the market.

As with so many other selling strategies, there are benefits and risks to backup offers. On the positive side, having a backup offer could make negotiations with your primary buyer go a bit more smoothly. For example, if the primary buyer knows there's someone waiting for the house if the deal falls through, they might ask for fewer concessions on repairs and other issues that might arise. Additionally, having a backup offer certainly can make it easier to deal with losing the primary buyer, since you have another buyer ready to step in.

On the other hand, you don't want to accept a backup offer solely to pressure your primary buyer. If the primary buyer cancels the deal, you don't want to be stuck with a significantly inferior backup offer from a risky buyer. Be sure to scrutinize any potential backup offer just as closely as you do your primary offer. To determine if a backup offer is worthwhile, ask yourself, Would I

What If It Doesn't Sell?

Believe it or not, sometimes houses just don't sell promptly or attract an acceptable offer. We've tried thus far to help you avoid this situation, but occasionally things don't go as smoothly as you would like. It's possible that mistakes were made, but more likely the market just went flat or some other innocuous quirk just got in the way. The most obvious remedy to the problem is to lower the listing price, but before you consider settling for less money there are other strategies to try.

You Can't Change the Location . . . or Can You?

You've probably heard the three most important factors in real estate are "location, location, location" or "You can change the house, but you can't change the location." Well, that's not exactly true; there are a few things you can do to improve your home's surroundings. Is your neighbor sabotaging your sale, with a messy yard and a dilapidated house? You might want to consider offering to clean up the yard, pay for more frequent garbage removal, or maybe even have the outside of his house painted.

Did you suddenly notice all of the traffic noise just after you put your house on the market? Fountains are great at minimizing traffic noise.

Unfortunately, there's only so much you can do to improve your location, and you may ultimately have to compensate for an imperfect setting by adjusting your price. But do everything you can, and see our suggestions below before you do.

Has Your House Become Your Home Again?

We know how exhausting and inconvenient it can be to keep your house in market-ready condition for an extended period of time. As time passes, sellers become a bit less diligent, letting some dishes pile up in the sink, leaving a few things here and there on the bathroom counter, or not fluffing the pillows with quite the same vigor as they did when the house first went on the market. We've had clients ask us, like despondent teenagers, "Do I really have to keep making my bed every day?" The answer, we're sorry to say, is yes. In fact, you may even need to be *more* diligent. As your house remains on the market, it can easily become "shelf stale," failing to generate that same enthusiasm it did early on. You need to keep the house perfectly clean, refresh all the flowers and plants, and continue staging it as a "model" home. Remember, the fiftieth buyer who walks through your door should be treated to the same ideal experience as the first one.

Check Your Agent's Activity

If you are at all concerned that not enough has been done to sell your house, you need to review the activity list that your agent proposed during your interview (see question 3 in "Top Ten Questions to Ask Prospective Agents" in Step 2). Has there been a brokers' open house? How many other open houses have been held? How many people have visited the house? Is there a lockbox so buyers can easily see the house? Have there been ads in the local paper? Is there a virtual tour available online? Has your agent promoted the listing at office meetings?

If you are dissatisfied with any of the answers you get, try to work with your agent

continued

to increase or focus her activity. If your concerns are not addressed sufficiently, it may be time to find a new agent. But once again, it could be the price.

Did We Mention That It Could Be the Price?

Sellers are understandably hesitant to reduce their asking price, but more often than not it is overpricing that prevents a house from selling. Sometimes sellers just priced the house too high from the beginning, but oftentimes the house was originally priced correctly but over time the market has changed. We find that sellers start to get anxious after about sixty days on the market, and a lot can change during that time. You may think that your homework ends once your house goes on the market, but you really need to keep up with market conditions, particularly if you sense that the market is cooling. Continue reading your local Real Estate section and keep going to open houses to check on the competition. Review new local listings and recent sales with your agent, and pay close attention to the market time for those listings. Increasing market time is a good indicator of a slowing market.

Ultimately, you need to be honest with yourself. If market conditions are clearly slowing and you've done everything you can to get your house in prime showing condition and it's still not selling, the time has probably come to lower the price. As when you set your listing price the first time, your new price should be based on recent sales of comparable homes. If the market seems stable, you may need to reconsider exactly what a comparable home is (this is where that brutal honesty comes in handy). In the case of a cooling market, you want to pay particular attention to the most recent sales. Work with your agent to get a sense of just how much the market is changing, and set the new price accordingly. And don't forget to consider your goals.

Remember Your Goals

If the time has come to reduce your price, it's also a good time to remember your goals. Sellers often let their pride get in the way of doing what's necessary to sell their homes, but reminding yourself of the goals you set originally can help you stay grounded and focused on the big picture.

If your top goals do not include selling quickly, you may want to consider taking your house off the market. We realize that this can feel like an admission of defeat, but if the market is changing and you don't have to sell right away, you may want to wait it out for a while. It's obviously not an ideal outcome, but taking your house off the market may help you make the best of a bad situation. If carrying costs are an issue, just be sure to calculate how much the delay will cost you.

accept this offer if the primary offer didn't exist? If the answer is no, you probably shouldn't designate it as a backup offer. In that case, you'll likely be better off putting the house back on the market.

You should also take market conditions into account when considering backup offers. In an improving market, you'll probably be better off putting the house back on the market if the first buyer falls through. In a softening market, a backup offer could help protect you against relisting in an even softer market in the future.

The Sales Agreement

The purpose of the sales agreement is to lay out the details of the sale, while protecting you financially (as well as emotionally). Your ultimate goal is to make sure that the sale is completed successfully and to specify all of the requirements that you and the buyer must complete before closing the sale and transferring the property. If the buyer does not perform according to the terms of the contract, a properly written sales agreement will ensure that you are adequately compensated. Remember, if this sale falls through, it doesn't affect just the timing of your move. It is also likely to negatively affect your eventual sale price. (See "Setting the Listing Price" in Step 2 for more information on what hap-

Offers from buyers who show less commitment (lower deposit and/or down payment) are riskier for sellers.

NO-BRAINER

pens when your house has to go back on the market.)

We feel that it is definitely useful for all sellers to be familiar with the basic components of the sales agreement. With this knowledge, you can bring up any specific concerns or details pertaining to you and the buyer so that each agent can tailor the agreement to meet everyone's particular needs.

There are so many different sales agreements throughout the country, it would be impossible to address all the details of every one. But you should be aware of the major points included in most every agreement. Keep in mind that you might encounter slightly different terminology in your particular contract, but these basic concepts should be included in virtually all sales agreements.

Price   Hopefully this figure warms your heart and sends visions of early retirement dancing through your head. Just don't allow a high offer price to blind you to other flaws that can cause trouble down the road (see "Contingencies" opposite).

Initial Deposit (aka Earnest Money Deposit)   Generally speaking, you want the buyer to put down as large a deposit as possible. It not only indicates just how serious and financially capable the buyers are, but if the deal does fall through you'll want the maximum possible financial remuneration to compensate you for lost time and possible impact on your home's market value. The buyer and seller usually negotiate the size of the initial deposit in the sales agreement, and some states have an industry standard percentage.

Total Down Payment   This amount gives you the best indication of the buyer's financial health and the likelihood of a smooth transaction. Obviously, buyers who offer smaller down payments (10 percent or less) have to take out larger mortgages, which are more difficult to qualify for and are more likely to fall through. This is when it is important to look closely at the buyer's prequalification letter and financial statements. Make sure you carefully consider all the details of offers with smaller down payments before accepting them.

Seller Financing   This can be rather complicated, but under certain circumstances it can be an excellent option for sellers. In this situation, the seller effectively acts as the mortgage lender for all or part of the mortgage, receiving a set payment schedule from the buyer based on an agreed-upon interest rate. This option would probably be most appealing to downsizers who have paid off houses with significant equity. If you're considering seller financing, be sure to talk with your agent and your accountant to determine if it actually is the best strategy for you.

Contingencies   This is where it gets interesting. Contingencies are tasks that must be completed within a certain time frame that buyers and sellers specify within the agreement, so that certain things get done and criteria get met before the transaction is completed. Although many contingencies are included to protect the buyers—it seems as if buyers have countless opportunities to back out of the deal, whereas sellers have precious few—they are also essential to the sellers as well. Here are the most common contingencies that you're likely to encounter:

1. *Appraisal contingency.* The appraisal is important to everyone involved in the transaction, as it can seriously affect the

buyer's financing. If the appraisal determines that your home's value is lower than the buyer's offer, that buyer will have more difficulty securing a mortgage. An appraisal contingency can appeal to buyers by protecting them from overpaying for the house.

In extremely hot markets, it's quite possible that the final sales price will be well above the listed price, and the appraisal will not meet that sales price. You don't want to be in a situation in which the buyer suddenly can't get the mortgage or must pay the difference between the appraised value and the sale price in cash. This buyer could possibly back out unless you're willing to lower the price, which unfortunately might be your best strategy at that point. To avoid this, some agents and sellers ask the buyer to eliminate the appraisal contingency during very hot sellers' markets.

2. *Loan contingency.* The vast majority of home buyers need to take out a mortgage to finance the purchase of a home, so for those folks it is patently obvious that if they can't get financing they can't buy the house. A loan contingency simply says that buyers won't be bound by the sales agreement if they can't secure financing. For sellers, it is essential to make sure there is a short time frame for this contingency, so that you can know as soon as possible that the buyer can actually secure the funds to buy your house. For example, a loan contingency might state that buyers have twenty-one days to present evidence of their formal loan approval. Keep in mind that the most serious buyers will have a prequalification letter from a lender that they will include when they submit their offer. Sellers should be wary when entertaining offers without a prequalification letter.

3. *Inspection contingencies.* Most buyers will opt to have a home inspection, and of those some will request that defects either be fixed by the seller or that money be credited back to them to fix those defects. The most important thing about the inspec-

tion is that it be done early in the process, so you have time to address any problems. In hot markets some buyers will waive the home inspection to make their offer more appealing. Remember that there are many inspections that the buyer can do, so you'll probably need to allow one to two weeks for this contingency to be satisfied.

4. Buyer's sale of previous home. This can be a land mine if not handled properly. As the name suggests, buyers will include this contingency to make sure that they can sell their current house before they are required to complete the transaction of buying yours. This contingency adds a new level of uncertainty to the process, and it's something over which you have no control. To make matters even worse, the buyers and sellers can line up like dominos, such that the sale of your buyers' house is contingent on their buyers' selling their house, and so on back down the line. If any one of those contingencies is not met, it will ripple through the chain of deals, ultimately scuttling yours. As you can see, this is a contingency you really want to avoid, if possible.

If you are seriously considering accepting an offer with this contingency, make sure your agent reviews the details of the listing for the buyer's current home to make sure that it is properly priced. Or, if the buyer's current house has already sold, your agent can review the purchase contract to make sure it looks like a solid transaction.

5. Seller's identification of new property. Of course, on the other side, if you're planning on buying a new home, you don't want to close on your current house until you have someplace to go. This contingency sets a time frame within which you can realistically expect to find a new property. This contingency is not terribly popular with buyers, so unless you're in a hot seller's market, expect to make some other concession if you need to include it.

As you can see, time is the crucial factor in most of these contingencies. Certain things need to get done within the specified amount of time for the buyer and seller to satisfy the requirements of the contract. If problems arise, you and your agent need to determine if it is best to amend the agreement to give the buyers more time, or cancel the agreement and move on.

You do have an option to give the buyers a written twenty-four-hour notice to perform or quit if they don't satisfy a particular contingency on time. This is an aggressive move, but it does put them on notice and clearly communicates that you are not fooling around. We usually issue one of these if we get even the slightest hint that the buyers are going to be dragging their feet. They must either shape up and start performing, or we'll quickly know that it's time to walk away.

Length of Escrow and Time to Closing   This part of the agreement sets the date for the closing, thus establishing the length of time both parties have to take care of all the details. We usually prefer that this time period be as short as possible, while still accommodating your needs to find another home, prepare to move out, and so forth. The reason to keep it short is that the longer you wait, the more likely it is that something could go wrong. For example, interest rates might go up and suddenly the buyer has not secured her ideal financing. She exercises her loan contingency and cancels the sale, and you suddenly find your house back on the market again.

If you absolutely must have a long escrow period, you may want to consider closing sooner and renting back from the buyers. Of course, if you do rent back there's a good chance the rent will be based on your buyers' carrying costs, which are likely to be much higher than yours since their new mortgage will probably be higher (and hopefully much higher) than your current one.

Inclusions and Exclusions   This part of the contract spells out in detail exactly what is included in the sale and what isn't. In other words, what are you leaving behind and what are you taking with you? As a general rule, if it is physically attached to the house, it stays. For example, wall-to-wall carpeting, light fixtures, faucets, built-in appliances, and attached bookcases. If there's anything in your house that should be included in the sale but you want to keep, you should remove and replace it ahead of time rather than making it an exclusion in the sales agreement. Regardless of how small the item, allowing you to keep it is a concession in the minds of buyers, and they'll rightly expect something in return.

Also, don't be intimidated by buyers who ask for everything. When we're representing buyers, that's exactly what we do. We figure that our clients won't get anything without asking for it, and the worst the sellers can do is say no. So don't be afraid to counter unreasonable requests for inclusions.

Sign, Sign, Everywhere You Sign   Remember, once you sign the sales agreement, the property really comes off the market. It is essential to your bottom line that this deal goes to closing. Make sure you're comfortable with the major points of the agreement, and discuss any questions or concerns with your agent.

THE CLOSING PROCESS

For many sellers, and particularly those with good agents, the closing process is a relatively quiet part of selling a house. Hopefully the only activity will be a few phone calls and a handful of

Title Search

The title search is one of the more mysterious disclosures. Basically, the title confers ownership of the property (and in particular the land). The buyers want to be sure that nobody can claim to hold the title after they've bought the property. A title search checks to make sure that the title is "clean" and that nobody will challenge the new buyer for ownership. Given that the land's ownership can go back hundreds of years, it's difficult to say with absolute certainty that the title is clean. Title insurance protects against this possibility.

BUZZWORD

straightforward decisions regarding any negotiating points. Beyond that, the most difficult part about the closing for sellers is signing that huge stack of legal documents without succumbing to a nasty case of writer's cramp. But behind the scenes, many different parties are working feverishly to make sure everything is in place so that all you have to do is show up and start signing. It is our job as agents to keep that circus running smoothly and on time, and to address any issues that can (and always do) arise at any time along the way.

Once the sales agreement is signed, the house is taken off the market and the closing process begins. Here in California this is referred to as the "escrow period," since an independent escrow company serves as the repository for the documents and monetary deposits that change hands during preparations for the transfer of ownership. In other states, sellers may hire a lawyer to facilitate the process. Regardless of who does what, the process usually involves the same basic steps.

Disclosures

As we'll see below when we chat with a real estate lawyer, completely disclosing any defect that might be of interest to a buyer is essential to a successful sale. The process clearly protects buyers by making sure they have as complete a picture as possible of the condition of the house they are about to purchase. As you can imagine, this step can get quite involved and result in any number of negotiating points.

The Appraisal

The buyer's bank needs to appraise the property to make sure it is of sufficient value to make the loan. As we mentioned above, the appraisal of your house can have a significant impact on the success of your sale. If the appraised value comes in lower than a buyer's offer, it's possible that the buyer will be unable to get a mortgage, and the deal will fall through. To minimize the chances of this happening, there are a few things you can do to help maximize the appraised value of your house. But first, let's explain exactly what an appraisal is (and what it isn't).

An appraisal is a detailed estimate of the current market value of your home. State-licensed professional appraisers try to develop as accurate an estimate as possible. Are they perfect? Of course not. Appraisals are sort of like those gas mileage estimates that the EPA puts on new cars. Those estimates are developed under ideal conditions and don't take into account the reality of normal driving. Appraisers can't possibly estimate every nuance of market conditions and the unique appeal of your house. Regardless, appraisals are important because some very important people, namely mortgage lenders, believe they are important.

So, how do you get your house to appraise for top dollar? First, treat the appraiser like a prospective buyer. Make sure your house is in the same condition as when it was on the market.

Remember, too, that appraisers are busy people. They need to understand what's so valuable about your house. Many times agents accompany appraisers as they conduct the appraisal to point out special features of the house. Plan to leave the house when the appraiser arrives. Often sellers feel that they need to point out every single thing that they think is special about the house, but many of the things that are important to the seller are not considered important information to the appraiser.

The Inspections

In most cases the buyer will have the house inspected, and if the buyer chooses, any issues that arise will need to be addressed. Beyond the general home inspection, the most common and important type is the termite inspection. Be sure to talk with your agent to interpret the results of this inspection. For example, out here in California, it's hard to find a house that doesn't have termites. Fortunately, the most common type of termite out here is relatively harmless and can be eliminated easily. In other parts of the country, a discovery of termites can be a major problem.

The Loan

Hopefully your buyer submitted a commitment letter from their bank along with their offer, so if the appraisal is acceptable the loan should go through without any delays. Your agent should check in with the buyer's agent or lender to make sure everything is moving along according to schedule.

The Closing

In California, closings are pretty uneventful. All of the documents are signed in advance and the closing just marks the time when the transfer of ownership is recorded in the new buyer's name. In other parts of the country, the buyer and seller will meet in a lawyer's office to sign all of the documents. If lawyers are involved where you live, we obviously recommend that you get your own lawyer rather than using the same one as your buyer. Once everything is signed, you just hand over the keys and the house effectively changes hands. (The transfer is not legally effective until the new deed is recorded at the county recorder's office, usually a few hours later or possibly even the next day.)

Scheduling the Closing   There are a couple important issues to consider when scheduling your closing. First, the buyer probably won't want to schedule the closing for a Monday. Because the buyer usually can't fund his loan and close on the same day, the loan would have to fund on the previous Friday. In that case the buyer would end up paying an extra two days on the principle and interest on the loan before actually closing on the house.

You should also avoid closing on a Friday, since it's common for last-minute problems to arise. Neither you nor the buyer will want to wait through the weekend to close. Remember, if the closing is delayed and one party is to blame, the other party may request a daily payment to cover the carrying costs. Since the buyer's mortgage is probably larger than yours, paying his carrying costs can add up to quite a lot of money.

If you're not moving into a new house immediately after closing, or you just can't completely move out before the closing, it is possible to have a grace period of a day or two written into the contract or to arrange for a longer-term "rent-back" of the property from the buyer. We only recommend this as a last resort, since you may need to pay the buyer a significant fee and if something were to go wrong during that time the legal ramifications could be messy.

Donna: All this stuff about scheduling the closing might seem like an afterthought to the whole process, but it's really important.

Shannon: Especially if the timing doesn't work out perfectly. Not only can it cost you money, as we've said, but it can also be incredibly stressful.

Donna: We've heard horror stories about sellers showing up to the closing in the moving van because they just finished packing moments before, or one seller who packed away his house keys and couldn't find them to give to the buyer.

Shannon: Do yourself (and your agent) a favor, and write up a schedule for the closing just like we did for the overall process back in Step 1. Start at the closing date and time and work backward through all of the packing and arrangements to move out.

The Lawyer

If you're lucky, you'll never meet Steven Spierer, a real estate lawyer in Southern California. It's nothing personal—Steve is a great guy with extensive real estate experience. He frequently speaks to agent organizations and other real estate groups, and he hosts an extremely informative radio show called *House Calls* (see "Resources for Sellers"). It's just that if you do meet Steve, it probably means you're involved in a lawsuit. If that's the case, just make darn sure Steve is on your side. The only thing worse than meeting the buyers in court is meeting the buyers in court and seeing Steve Spierer sitting next to them.

To make sure this never happens to you, we sat down with Steve and asked him what gets sellers into trouble and how they can stay out of his office.

D&S: All right, Steve, let's start off with the big one: what's the most common mistake sellers make that gets them in trouble?

Steve: Failure to fully disclose probably accounts for about 85 percent of lawsuits. In the old days it was caveat emptor, or buyer beware. Basically, the buyers were primarily responsible for uncovering any potential issues with a property. These days, it's caveat vendor, or seller beware. The onus is definitely on the seller to disclose any and all possible issues to the buyer.

D&S: What kinds of things should sellers disclose?

Steve: Sellers should disclose any and all defects that could be of even the slightest interest to a buyer. And the more you'd rather not disclose something, the more likely it is to be something you should disclose.

D&S: So you recommend that sellers disclose everything?

Steve: Yes. Sellers should disclose and disclose and then disclose some more. When you get to the point where you've disclosed so much that you think the buyer couldn't possibly still want to buy your house, then you've disclosed enough.

D&S: We're glad you said it, because we often see clients getting a little nervous when we get aggressive with the disclosures.

Steve: In fact, that should make them more comfortable. The sellers who should be nervous are the ones whose agents start playing around with disclosures. If your agent will lie to the other side, he'll lie to you, too.

D&S: While we're talking about agents, what's your advice for sellers who want to sell themselves?

Steve: This actually relates to the second most common mistake that I see sellers make: overestimating their own talent. I buy and sell real estate all the time, and I've been a real estate lawyer for more than thirty years. I can say with some confidence that I know a lot about real estate. I *always* work with an agent (a Realtor, in fact), just as when I need surgery I always get a doctor. Sellers without agents are really just out to sea, adrift in the dark.

D&S: There's a lot of talk about how sellers can access so much information online. Is it possible for sellers to learn what they need to know to successfully represent themselves?

Steve: I hear all the time that sellers can find almost everything they need to know online. That may be so, but looking for important information online is like the drunk looking for his car keys beneath a streetlight. He's not likely to find his keys there, but he looks there since that's where the light is. The point is, just because there's a lot of information online, that doesn't mean it's the right information, or even that it's true.

D&S: Is there a middle ground? What about the emerging market for discount brokers?

Steve: This is another common mistake that often gets sellers into trouble. They want to save a few dollars and can't imagine what the difference could be between a discount agent and a full-fee, professional

agent. I can imagine the difference, and I work to remedy the results of it all the time. As I see it, discount agents charge less because they believe that they're worth less than other agents. Sellers should believe them.

D&S: We discussed the value of good agents earlier, but can you give an example of a way that an experienced, professional agent can keep people out of trouble?

Steve: Fear causes some sellers to make poor choices. They understandably get nervous that they'll scare buyers away by disclosing too much, or they worry that if they cancel a sale to a nonperforming buyer they'll never find another one. Without the guidance and advice of a good agent, sellers are prone to negotiate from a position of fear rather than with a sense of opportunity.

D&S: And what happens then?

Steve: Fear can cause sellers to ignore the warning signs. If a buyer isn't performing, you don't want fear to prevent you from taking appropriate action. Sometimes you need to say, "Take it or leave it," which feels risky but in these cases is actually safer. Fearful sellers will stick with an underperforming buyer (which feels safe but is actually riskier). Sometimes they even make unnecessary concessions to keep the

WORDS FROM THE WISE

buyer, who then starts asking for more and more until the transaction becomes a nightmare.

Ultimately, you need to balance all of the possible outcomes, both good and bad, and heed the warning signs along the way. It's like driving through a yellow light. Sure, you can speed up through the inter-section, and most of the time you'll be fine. But if you slow down and stop, in the long run you'll have fewer accidents and get fewer tickets.

D&S: Any other pearls of wisdom?

Steve: If you think you need to consult a lawyer, you probably do.

WORDS FROM THE WISE

Let's Talk Taxes

We put it off as long as possible, but the time has come to talk about that incessant little inconvenience we all love to hate: taxes. Before we begin, let us just preface this discussion by strongly advising you to work with a professional accountant. Once you become a homeowner, your taxes get sufficiently complicated to justify the expense of an accountant (in many cases an accountant will cover his or her fee by uncovering many ways to lower your tax burden). When you sell your house, an accountant is absolutely indispensable. And under no circumstances should you allow this book to substitute for professional tax advice. We're just providing you with an overview so you'll know what to expect when you do sit down with a pro.

Luckily for you, selling your house is one of the few times that there is actually good news to be found in the tax code, so let's get right to it. There is really only one major tax issue that affects sellers (of course, everyone's situation is unique, and there may be other issues that you and your accountant will need to address). CPAs everywhere lovingly refer to it as Internal Revenue Code (IRC) section 121.

You may also hear about section 1031 or "in-kind exchanges," but that only pertains to the sale of investment property. If you are selling such a property, definitely consult a tax professional.

IRC Section 121—Exclusion of Gain from Sale of Primary Residence   The Taxpayer Relief Act of 1997 allows you to exclude from your taxable income a sizable amount of the capital gains from the sale of your primary residence. Single taxpayers can exclude up to $250,000 and married couples filing jointly can exclude up to $500,000 of the gain they realize on the sale. Any gains above that are taxed at the appropriate capital gains tax rate.

According to the law, for your house to be considered your primary residence you must have owned it for at least two years (this is known as the "ownership test") and it must have been your primary residence for at least forty-eight of the past sixty months (the "use test"). You may qualify for an exception to these rules if you are forced to relocate for a job, for health reasons, or because of other unforeseen circumstances. In these cases, you would qualify for a partial exclusion, depending on how long you lived in your house before selling. One additional rule you must meet to qualify for the exclusion is that you must not have excluded gains on the sale of another house within the past two years.

So, assuming you qualify for a section 121 exclusion, how do you determine your exact capital gain on the sale? The answer is simple (sort of): your capital gain is equal to the difference between the "cost basis" of your house and its sales price. Now you have to know what a cost basis is and how to calculate it for your house.

The cost basis is the net cost of the house to you since you purchased it. Here's how you calculate your cost basis:

- Start with the purchase price that you paid for your home.

- Add any closing costs from your purchase and sale of the home.

- Add the cost of any capital improvements you made to the house.

- Capital improvements add to the long-term value of your house. They do not include maintenance like painting or general repairs.

It may seem like a simple equation, but calculating it correctly can get complicated. And the outcome can result in significant tax savings. Now you see why we adamantly recommend hiring an accountant.

The Deal Is Done

We mentioned earlier that closings in California tend to be pretty anticlimactic. The paperwork is compiled and signed well in advance, and the transaction is simply finalized on a set date. While it's an efficient and relatively stress-free way to close, sometimes we wish we were a part of those closings where the buyers and sellers get together and transfer ownership of the house with a dramatic flourish of signatures.

For any closing, sellers really feel the weight of the transaction as they reach the end of this major chapter in the process. There's the joy and pride of a job well done, then there's the relief of no longer being sellers, and finally there's the realization that a new exciting (and potentially unnerving) transition lies ahead.

In fact, by the time you reach the closing on your house, that transition is already well under way. It started when you began packing up your house and started preparing yourself to move out. In the days leading up to the closing, your soon-to-be ex-home undoubtedly will be caught in a maelstrom of packing, cleaning, and countless logistical nightmares. You may even have the added excitement of buying a new house at the same time. To help you stay calm during this storm, and make it to the closing with some sanity left, let's step back a bit and figure out how to manage the move from the beginning.

Move Out, Move In, Move On

BESIDES ALL OF THE all of the activities directly related to selling your home, there are two other major undertakings that you're likely to face during this time: moving and buying your new house. We could write a whole other book about buying a home, but just as a quick introduction to the process, let's revisit some of the things we've already talked about in this book that can also make you a better buyer.

Setting goals as a buyer can help you refine your search and stay within your means.

Understanding what kind of buyer you are can help you understand what's most important to you and set a reasonable schedule.

Finding the right agent can help you navigate the process, stay focused, and find out what's really the best house for you.

Getting your finances in order is essential.

Understanding the local market can help you recognize when a house is priced properly and when it's not.

Since you now know everything a seller should do, you can recognize when those things aren't done. From the buyer's side, any money that the sellers leave on the table is yours.

Obviously, buying can be much more intimidating than selling since afterward you end up with a big mortgage rather than a big check. But you've also got a new house and a fresh start, and that can be priceless. Of course, before you can start your wonderful new life, you've got to move out of your current house and into your new one. Moving may seem like a major chore that you just have to grind your way through, but there are steps you can take to help your move go a bit more smoothly.

The Mover

If there is a hell, we're pretty sure that the most nefarious souls are condemned to live out eternity moving from one house to the next. Imagine an endless sequence of packing and unpacking. It's too horrible to imagine. We asked Tom Myers of All-American Movers in Manhattan Beach, California, if there was anything he could recommend to make the process more bearable.

D&S: We absolutely hate moving. Besides the inconvenience of it all, you end up going through all your old stuff and being reminded of all the fashion and relationship mistakes you've made. Plus, we're usu-ally totally exhausted from all of the other craziness in life at that time; packing everything up is the last thing we want to do. How can we make it easier?

Tom: Everyone hates moving; in fact, it's right up there with marriage and the death of a loved one as the most stressful events in life. Probably the wisest thing to do to help minimize the stress is to start packing well in advance of your move. You both know how helpful it can be to clear out much of your stuff before your house goes on the market. In my experience it takes at least a month for normal, working people to pack up completely. Sure, you can do it in less time, but you'll be more stressed out.

D&S: So, waiting until the night before the movers arrive is probably not wise?

Tom: I can't tell you how many clients have canceled the day before because they've just started packing and realize they'll never be ready in time.

D&S: Assuming most people won't have enough time to pack, how can they do it as efficiently as possible?

Tom: Get organized. I would recommend that you buy your boxes from the movers. They'll be cheaper, and the movers should know exactly how many you'll need. Label all the boxes clearly (MB for master bedroom, LR for living room, etc.). Keep track of your labeling scheme, so that when you move in you can label each room accordingly and the movers will know where everything goes. Also, make sure you keep all of the special wrenches and fasteners you use for particular pieces of furniture. Just put them in a plastic bag and tape the bag to the furniture itself.

D&S: What about just leaving the packing for the movers?

Tom: Sure, you can do that, but it's going to cost you more money. Any move of less than one hundred miles within the same state is priced by the hour. You want to pay the movers to move things, not to disassemble a crib or keep track of the dog. Longer moves or moves between states are priced by weight, so in that case you might want to have the movers pack everything up.

Try to budget enough time to really get organized so that all the movers have to do is load boxes onto the truck. In particular, box up all that small stuff that you put away when you staged your house. Our job goes much more quickly if we can build walls of boxes in the truck. If we're loading individual lamps or loose pictures, we can't stack anything on top of them.

D&S: We're always afraid that we'll pack things improperly and they'll arrive in a thousand pieces.

Tom: One of the biggest problems we encounter is packing too much into too big a box. If you can't lift it, we can't lift it, and we're allowed to refuse to move something because of worker's comp laws. So, stick with mostly small and medium boxes. This will also make it easier for you to stack the boxes neatly in the garage to get them out of the way during showings.

Also, the best packing material is crumpled-up newspaper. If you're worried about the ink, your movers should be able to supply you with blank newsprint.

WORDS FROM THE WISE

Make sure every single piece is wrapped. You may have seen that trick where you squeeze an egg from top to bottom and it doesn't break. The same is true for dishes and other thin breakables. Wrap your dishes and stack them on their sides rather than on top of each other.

D&S: Now that you mentioned breakables, what's the deal with insurance? Is it worth buying?

Tom: All licensed movers offer basic insurance at no additional cost (actually, the cost is built into their price). This insurance is not meant to replace broken or lost items, since it only provides about $.60 per pound per item. Movers also offer full replacement coverage, and the price depends on the amount of coverage and the deductible.

Before you purchase additional insurance from your movers, read your homeowners' insurance policy. Just about every policy has moving insurance included in it, so you only need to buy insurance from the movers if you want additional coverage.

Just remember for something to be insured (except very large items) it needs to be boxed, and that means it's completely enclosed and taped.

D&S: That's great to know. What about advice for the other end of the move?

Tom: When you get into the new house, label each room with a Post-it note on the wall where you want the movers to stack all the boxes. That way they can get everything into the correct room and keep it out of the way so they can move the furniture in.

Also, make sure there's somebody around to answer questions, since it's much easier for the movers to move boxes around than for the homeowners to do it.

D&S: Any other advice for our intrepid sellers?

Tom: Box up valuables and electronics yourself, and set aside anything that you don't want packed away. Finally, please pack away any potentially embarrassing items. If your mother shouldn't see it, the movers shouldn't either.

WORDS FROM THE WISE

TAKE A MOMENT

We really hope you have a successful sale and that you meet or exceed all of your goals. When the whole process is complete and your house is officially sold, it can be a bit anticlimactic. You spend so much time preparing yourself and your house for the market, and distancing yourself emotionally, that it can be hard to celebrate when it's all over. Plus, there's the little inconvenience of actually moving, which tends to get in the way of the festivities. Do yourself a favor and try to set aside a brief moment of time to really appreciate what you've just accomplished. This is a major moment in your life and you don't want to let it slip by without acknowledging it.

SAYING OUR OWN GOOD-BYES

As much as we encourage our clients to distance themselves emotionally from the process of selling their homes, sometimes we have a hard time doing so ourselves. While we're always happy and proud to help our clients achieve their goals, it's hard to say good-bye. We get very attached to our clients, and coming to the end of a successful sale is always a bittersweet experience. Looking back at everything we've talked about in this book, we can understand why.

Selling a house is so much more than just a financial transaction, and sometimes we feel more like therapists than real estate agents. We work very hard to help our clients learn about themselves. We help them define their goals and tailor our approach to their individual personalities. Most sellers are going through major life transitions—happy changes like marriage or children or sad ones like divorce or a death in the family—and we learn virtually every de-

Your homeowners' insurance policy probably includes at least some movers' insurance.

INSIDER SECRET

tail about their private lives in the process. It's impossible for us not to become protective of our clients, to empathize with them and treat them like family. We spend so much time together and go through such deeply emotional times during the sale that we're often sad to see it end.

But with every sale, each ending is also a beginning. We work with clients over and over again across many years, and in some cases we find ourselves working with our clients' children as they move on and start families of their own. For you, our readers, we've strived to share everything with you and help you find success and fun every step along the way. We're very proud to have the opportunity to share our knowledge and experience with you, and we hope that the end of this book is also yet another beginning. We wish you all the best of luck and happy sales.

Resources for Sellers

American Institute of Architects Home Design Trends Survey

When you're considering home improvements, it's worth knowing what updates are the most in demand. That way, you'll be reasonably confident that the changes you make won't seem outdated or old fashioned if you sell in the not-too-distant future. Each year the AIA surveys hundreds of its member architects to find out what types of work their clients are asking them to do. The results can show you what home improvement trends are just emerging. Check out the latest survey results at their Web site, www.aia.org/econ_designsurvey_results.

American Society of Home Inspectors

Yes, home inspectors are still underregulated, but this association aims to advance the professionalism of the field. Its Web site, www.ashi.org, offers a virtual home inspection that can give you a quick overview of the inspection process.

Annual Credit Report

You should regularly check your credit reports for errors, and you are allowed by law to view your report from each of the three major credit-reporting agencies once a year for free. To order your annual credit report, go to www.annualcreditreport.com.

Goodwill

To find a donation center near you, or to arrange for a pickup, go to www.goodwill.org or call 800-741-0186.

House Calls *Radio Show*

Hosted by Steven Spierer (see "Words from the Wise: The Lawyer" in Step 6), this call-in talk show airs on Saturdays from 10 a.m. — 12 p.m. Pacific daylight time, and covers all the hot topics on buying and selling real estate. Listen to archived shows and link to the live broadcast from 97.1 FM, www.971freefm.com.

Real Estate Words

This online glossary of real estate terms is a great resource for getting definitions of all the arcane terminology we real estate agents use all the time. Go to www.realestatewords.com to find out what they all mean.

ServiceMagic

This site helps you find local service people quickly and easily. All you do is submit a request for the work you want done, and the service people will contact you directly. You can also check reviews from other customers to make sure you're hiring a pro. To get started, go to www.servicemagic.com.

Zillow

Zillow uses a complex formula to estimate a home's current value. It is an excellent resource for getting a general sense of your list price, since it shows comparable homes in your neighborhood and also shows trends in prices. To take advantage of Zillow's free service, go to www.zillow.com.

Recommended Reading

Clutter's Last Stand: It's Time to De-Junk Your Life!
by Don Aslett
We love this book, which provides countless recommendations for organizing your stuff and your life.

Feng Shui: Arranging Your Home to Change Your Life
by Kirsten Lagatree
This is a wonderful book that provides an introduction to feng shui and explores its applications in your home. We included some of Kirsten's advice already (see "Words from the Wise: The Feng Shui Lady" in Step 5), but check out her book if you want to bring the principles of feng shui into your home.

Home Depot Home Improvement 1-2-3 and
Lowe's Complete Home Improvement and Repair
From simple fixes to more extensive renovations, both of these books provide instructions for just about any project around your house.

IRS Publication 523: "Selling Your Home"
If you want a thorough and surprisingly readable explanation of the tax consequences of selling your house, visit the Web site of the Internal Revenue Service at www.irs.gov and search for Publication 523.

Real Estate Journal:
The Wall Street Journal Guide to Property
This site makes it easy to keep up with national real estate trends, tax issues, and just about everything else you should know as a seller. Go to www.realestatejournal.com.

Taunton's Build Like a Pro Series
If you're planning to do any substantial remodeling yourself—tiling, remodeling a kitchen or bath, updating electrical or plumbing—these books offer clear and concise explanations of every step along the way.

Workbench Magazine
If you're a dedicated do-it-yourselfer, this magazine is an excellent resource to help you with woodworking projects specifically designed to improve your home. The instructions are straightforward and many of the projects present creative solutions to common household problems (especially storage).

Acknowledgments

We would like to thank the following people.

Clive Pearse, thank you for your constant support and never-ending belly laughs. You are our ambassador to this new world.

Paul Barrutia, we would not be here without you. We appreciate you more than you know.

Craig Boreth, thank you for your calm nature, dedication, and incredible writing. We feel so lucky to have worked with you on this book.

Laurie Abkemeier, Shana Drehs, and Mary Choteborsky, thank you for navigating us through this adventure.

We are also so appreciative of those who contributed to this book: Steven Spierer, Judy Smith, Kirsten Lagatree, Tom Myers, Paul Ferguson, and Frank Paine for the illustrations.

Jeremy Kaufman, thanks for the free office space and all those Diet Cokes.

Finally, to Jeffrey, who taught us to look at the big picture and never to step over the dimes to pick up the nickels. Thank you.

Index